Tickled Pink:

A Guide to Erotic Fun with Tickling

Christopher and Donna Benoit

Published by Laughing Gull Literature

Oceanside, NY

Table of Contents

Foreword

Foreword

This book is being co-written by a couple who enjoy erotic tickling as an aspect of their sexual play. In our relationship, Donna enjoys being tickled by Chris (and select others). Chris enjoys tickling Donna (and those same select others). We discovered our mutual interest as a result of sex play that came during the early, nervous exploration stage of our relationship, and we now use tickling in a variety of ways to supercharge our sex life.

Chris had already had some experience in the area of tickling and domination and submission (D & S) play by the time he met Donna. Donna was a bit more of a novice in this area, but with a writer's curiosity and all the imagination in the world.

Because this book is being co-authored by the two of us, the writing styles may appear to change slightly from section to section. We like to think of it as a narrative approach that will give the reader the best of both perspectives on tickling (the giver and the receiver).

We think it's important to mention at the outset that we do not support gender stereotypes in any type of power or other sex games. Usually in the "fetish" literature, women are portrayed as the submissive figures, while men are more dominant. Another popular portrayal is one woman dominating another. In reality, however, men often like to be submissive as well. All of the games and scenarios that we describe in this book are flexible and can accommodate either gender in any role. We've tried our best to be gender-unspecific in our descriptions.

We emphasize safety and consent throughout the book, so it seems proper that we do it once here during the foreword. Tickling can be tremendously fun and erotic, done properly. It can also be torturous and abusive, however, if done improperly. Safewords (the secret word that signals that one is moving past the point of endurance/pleasure) need to be employed so that limits are not exceeded. We suggest using a word that wouldn't ordinarily come up within the situation, for example "soap", so that the ticklee is free to beg and plead in keeping with his/her role but doesn't stop the activity unless truly in the danger zone. Alternatively, you can use a "green, yellow, red" system to indicate when activities are escalating too far.

You need to make sure that your partner is someone you can truly trust, since physical restraint is sometimes involved. In our opinion, gags should never be used, since they can cut the ability to breathe, an ability that is often already challenged by the tickling. They also prevent the use of the safeword and take away from the situation: hearing the laughing and pleading is half the fun! On a similar theme, bondage should never put pressure on your partner's neck and therefore challenging breathing.

If limits and safety are respected, the games that we describe here can give your sex life a real shot of power. Here's to hoping you create a nice ticklish situation!

Chapter 1: The Psychology of the Tickle

The dictionary defines tickling as an excitation of the surface nerves of the skin that causes spasmodic and uncontrollable laughter, squirming, and attempts to escape the stimulation. The dictionary also tells you interesting facts, such as not all people are ticklish and that you cannot tickle yourself. What the dictionary definition fails to address, however, is just how sexually exciting tickling can be.

Tickling can serve a variety of functions for sexual partners, depending on how it is used. It can be playful fun, a seemingly innocent icebreaker that allows intimate physical contact to begin between nervous partners, flirting, role-play (see the fantasy section), or even a domination and submission (D & S) game. Rueger (1981) describes erotic tickling (p. 166):

"You can get really worked up during a heavy bout of tickling. Not only do you blow off steam, but the intense, intimate touching can be quite sexually stimulating. Some ticklish areas are also very erotic. When you start playing with them, you're in the twilight zone between tickling and sex."

Tickling as a sexual activity has recently been

6

enjoying a surge of popularity. Although this is the first serious attempt at a book on the subject, tickling is the subject of a burgeoning "fetish" (actually, the correct term would be "paraphilia") film and magazine market. Tickling has been explored in numerous adult magazines (e.g., Forum, Variations, Penthouse, etc.), the popular Real Personal television program (on CNBC cable television), and even demonstrated several times on the Howard Stern radio/television program (on the E! Network). On Stern's program, two episodes were with willing tickling fans. In other episodes, television movie host Rhonda Shear ("USA Up All Night!") and musician Belinda Carlisle ("the Go-Gos") were tickled. Of all these episodes, only Belinda was not placed into bondage first. By the time of the Rhonda episode, Stern had engaged in so much tickling that a specially-made bondage device (colonial stocks that have been manufactured by the World Wide Tickling Club and dubbed the "laughing stocks") had been installed in his studio.

Tickling in these forums is usually discussed in terms of D & S play. One partner (usually the woman, or a woman since both tickler and ticklee are often women in the fetish market materials) is tied and tickled by the other. This is a playful form of sex

7

play where one partner can dominate the other without inflicting any real pain or physical damage, which are a turn-off for many. Love (1992) refers to the paraphilia of being sexually aroused by tickling as both "knismolagnia" and "titillagnia". Discussions of tickling, even in sexology books, are exceptionally rare, however.

In a future chapter, we discuss many sexual games with a tickling theme. In these games, the "victim" seems to be "tortured" by the other partner. The torture is playful, sensual domination without the "pain, whips and chains" most associate with D & S play.

"Tickling...excites some people out of their minds. For others it's agony but increases general arousal." The Joy of Sex.

In Volume 3 of Videos for Lovers: Behind the Bedroom Door (telephone 800-866-1000), we see both sides of the coin. In this video, bondage and tickling, as well as the appropriate sensitivity to your partner's feelings, are demonstrated by a young couple named Annie and Eric. Eric ties Annie and tickles her with a large feathery frond that he has found growing on the side of the road, challenging her

8

not to move while being stroked.

Before the actual tickling episode, we hear Eric talk about wanting to try this new game. Even though he himself doesn't like to be tickled, he thinks that Annie might. He was correct. After the game, Annie talks about how much she enjoyed being tied and tickled. They both agree, however, that although Eric doesn't mind activities such as being tied up or having his toes sucked, he can't stand to be tickled at all. Annie quotes Eric: "That was the big rule: NEVER, NEVER tickle me." To Eric, tickling is a self-described phobia, a form of torture.

Tickling as torture? It may seem silly to some, but open a discussion with a few friends. Mention an intention to tickle, and some will shrink back in absolute terror. It is common to hear experienced Domination and Submission (D & S) players admit to being able to stand any amount of pain, but to being reduced to using the safeword within seconds after tickling has begun. The unfortunate truth is that many people have had very bad experiences with tickling. Because it is not generally regarded as painful, people have no hesitation to tickle others, especially children, for prolonged periods.

Being tickled involves losing control. The tickled person may be unable to control his/her laughter and squirming, and may have trouble breathing normally. (S)he may not be able to stop the tickling due to being held, being smaller, or just because (s)he is weak from struggling. This leads to feelings of helplessness and panic and can be so traumatic that even as adults such people cannot bear even the thought of being tickled. This is indeed a pity, since tickling play with a partner who respects limits (and limits are often ever-expanding once trust is established) can be truly pleasurable. It is our hope that some people who currently dislike or even fear tickling will learn to try it, and come to enjoy it, as a result of this book.

If some learn to fear tickling, how do others learn to love it? One of the main theories regarding the development of fetishes, or even your run-of-the-mill "turn on," is classical conditioning. You remember, how Ivan Pavlov taught his doggies to salivate to the sound of a bell. The main point of classical conditioning is that something that was previously meaningless comes to take on great significance by being paired with something that is more naturally relevant.

So let's look at tickling: it begins as something neutral. But when you tickle someone, let's say on the ribs, (s)he may squirm into you. This can be quite physically stimulating, and possibly sexually arousing. Suddenly the sounds of the laughter and begging and squirming become associated with sexual arousal (which, if carried on long enough, can often lead to orgasm). This is how many ticklers report developing their interest: by having tickling paired with sexual arousal caused by the frenzied physical contact. Don't forget that the tickled person is also experiencing the same physical stimulation, so (s)he is also every bit as likely to suddenly look at tickling in a whole new light.

There is also a psychology at work here. Many who enjoy sexual dominance also find an erotic element of power in this situation (thus the inclusion of a small tickling section in Scott's Erotic power: An exploration of dominance and submission). Someone who is a bit more sexually submissive and being tickled may become aroused by this new type of domination and is also a prime candidate for considering tickling a major turn-on. As alluded to earlier, tickling can serve many functions for the dominant and submissive:

1. creating feelings of helplessness and tension with proper technique (e.g., blindfolds, tickling and then massaging and then tickling again, verbal teasing, etc.),

2. serving as something to offer as an expression of

trust and devotion ("I place my bare feet in your lap to do with as you see fit"),

3. as a tool to "force" a partner to negotiate out of a ticklish situation (see the game play chapter), and

4. as a "punishment" for inappropriate behavior ("I warned you about doing that, and now you're going to get tickled").

All of this makes tickling a perfect activity for exploring dominant and submissive urges.

While tickling is very often explored in the context of domination and submission games, including bondage, it need not be used that way. Of all the movie tickling scenes described in chapter 5, only two involve bondage. If you wait until your partner is tied up to tickle, you'll be wasting many opportunities for spontaneous fun. Tickling is meant to be playful and suggestive. Use it to get under your partner's skin and to let him/her know that you want to play, or use it to tease your partner to build tension for later. Look for your opportunities to get in those spontaneous (sneaky?) tickles. Some suggestions:

1. Your partner is pulling a shirt over his/her head. Go for those ribs!

2. Help your partner on with his/her shoes and sneak in a tickle on the feet.

3. Your partner reaches up to change a light bulb or

get an item from a high shelf. You know the rest.

4. Your partner is laying on the bed or couch reading. A tickle on the foot will draw attention away from the book directly to you.

5. Start a tickle wrestling match (see chapter 2).

6. Your partner is driving. Get in a quick tickle just as the light is about to change from red to green. (S)he won't have time to get you back. This can be repeated at the next light, and suddenly driving takes on a whole new dimension. When you and your partner finally get home, however, don't say we didn't warn you if you get attacked (in any number of ways).

Once you begin to link tickling with your sex play, delivering a tickle to your partner will let him or her know that you're in the mood for fun. Soon, via that wonderful process of classical conditioning, the initial tickle delivered by either one of you will turn you both on.

Tickling and Anthropology

There is a scarcity of information regarding how tickling has been combined with sexuality across cultures. We were able to find only a few such references. Love (1992) details two examples: Bagandan women used underarm tickling as a seduction technique. She also references Goldberg's anthropological treatise, The Sacred Fire: The Story

13

of Sex in Religion, which describes a sect of Russian men who tickled women as a part of religious ceremonies (and were therefore known as "The Ticklers"). In The Sex Life of the Foot and Shoe, Rossi (1978) makes other references to Czarist Russia and tickling games engaged in by the women of the aristocracy. Some servants became especially prized for their ability to physically and verbally tease their mistresses (sounds like a dream job to some people we know). This practice was supposedly the inspiration for the bondage and tickling scene near the outset of the film version of The Brothers Karamazov (see favorite movie scenes). In the novel itself there is a discussion of the ticklishness of a man's wife, and how he was moved to violence at the thought of another man tickling her. In the movie, Great Catherine, the actress playing the Russian Czarina Catherine the Great ties and tickles her lover, again supposedly as a tribute to the sexual practice of the time.

Historical tickle torture

Tickling was supposedly also practiced as a torture/punishment by the Spanish Inquisition (rumored to be associated especially with Friar Tomaso). Tickling was reported to be among the many tortures used to extract confessions by the inquisitors. Colonial American settlers were also supposed to have employed this torture. Prisoners were trapped in the stocks and their feet were tickled with feathers or by animal lickings. Whether this is true or not, there was nothing even remotely sexual about this torture as it was practiced. Still, that shouldn't stop you from incorporating such ideas into historical fantasy play (see Chapter 3).

Have Fun

As a final note, it's no accident that the word "play" is contained within "foreplay." When was the last time you tickled your partner? Why so long? Laughter is a great way to recover from stress and to break tension. Rather than yelling at a spouse, how about challenging a tickle wrestle, or threatening to tickle? Won't you both feel better? Tickling, if not colored by traumatic experience, is generally reported as a pleasurable experience. Allowing yourself to laugh, to trust, and to just generally have a good time are some of the healthiest things you can do for your sex life. It can also inject new spirit into your relationship in general. ENJOY!!!

Chapter 2:   Tickling Techniques

When considering tickle techniques, there are two main questions: where to tickle, and how to tickle. As to the question of where, of course it depends upon the individual.   Though there is some debate on this point, it does seem that some people, unfortunately, just aren't ticklish.   No amount of tickling can make the not-ticklish individual so much as smile.   Of course, many people claim not to be ticklish.   Most are lying.   Never take someone's word for it, and be persistent (but also be sensitive, some people really don't like tickling and may be lying for this reason, perhaps due to some prior aversive conditioning).   Five seconds of tickling may be tolerated without response. Five minutes won't be.   Also, some people who are not normally ticklish may become sensitive when sexually excited or when put in a vulnerable position, like being tied up and/or blindfolded.

So why are some people ticklish, and not others? Nobody really knows.   Biologists believe that the nerves that transmit tickle messages from the skin to the brain are the same ones that transmit pain messages (the so-called "C fibers":   Leuba, 1941).   If this is true, it makes it a little easier to understand why some people find tickling so unpleasant.

While some people report that their general

ticklishness changes over time, most people report that their ticklishness is fairly stable. Researchers Fridlund and Loftus, in the journal Biological Psychology, have noted that the reaction to tickle stays fairly consistent across time. They also describe a correlation between ticklishness and the tendency to blush, as well as other autonomic nervous system reactions. They also suggest that there may be some degree of familial inheritance of ticklishness. Despite all of this information, just what separates a ticklish person from a not ticklish person on the biological level is still a mystery.

Most people who are ticklish and who do not enjoy it as an aspect of their sexual play will tell you that they would rather not be ticklish at all. They regard it as a vulnerability, a weakness, and often a means of being dominated or even humiliated by another (small wonder that many lash out, almost in a panic, when tickled). Why would nature build such a "vulnerability" into the biology of the person? Surely there must be some pay-off that makes this extra sensitivity worth having.

It was Charles Darwin in The Expression of Emotion in Man and Animals who first suggested that ticklishness might serve some evolutionary purpose. Darwin (see Science Digest, August 1984) noted that the

17

parts of the body that tend to be the most ticklish are also the spots that tend to have the thinnest skin and are generally the most vulnerable from the physical threats (e.g., insects) that existed when humans lived in more primitive conditions. That extra bit of sensitivity might make the difference between life and death from such a physical threat.

The tickle sensation is obviously complicated for the brain to process. Japanese researcher Takahashi Hoshikawa has detailed that whether or not the brain will register a touch as a tickle depends on the context of the touch. The same touch delivered by a doctor during an examination may not be experienced as a tickle, but it is more likely to be processed as a tickle if delivered by a lover. Also, there is the old paradox that most people believe it is impossible to tickle yourself (see the research article by Claxton noted in the reference section). The same physical sensation delivered by another is a tickle, but only a neutral touch if delivered by one's own hand.

Why should who is doing the touching matter? Perhaps relaxation is the issue. Books for massage therapists, for example, note that a relaxed body is less ticklish than a more tense one. Still, no amount of relaxation helps some people to avoid feeling ticklish on their most sensitive spots. Italian researcher Vezio Ruggieri and his colleagues have noted that some psychological factors seem to be associated with ticklishness (for example, cerebral dominance and body acceptance). Still, a theory that would explain why some are ticklish and not others, or why some people are ticklish in some spots and not others, is lacking. Clearly, we're dealing with a very complicated set of sensations.

To test out a prospective partner's ticklishness, the usual spots to try are:

1. The feet. Don't just think about the soles of the feet. The tops and sides can be very sensitive, especially where the top of the foot blends into the shin, and the outside of the foot, just under the ankle, as it fades into the heel. Light scraping and flicking motions with fingernails seem to work best here. The toes, just at the base, at the tips, and in between, can be truly stimulating. Use light scratching, kneading or licking/sucking here. A feather or artist brush between the toes can also be very stimulating.

2. The knees. Behind the knees is great for fingernail scrapes and playful licking, while the tops and sides of the kneecaps are great for kneading. This spot is sometimes the most ticklish on the body.

3. The stomach, sides, underarms, and ribs are great

for scrapes and gentle probes.

4. <u>The neck and ears</u> are great for scrapes and licks.

5. <u>The back</u> is great for scrapes, especially right down the spine and down near the kidneys.

6. <u>The buttocks</u> are great for scrapes.

Rueger (1981) breaks ticklish spots down into three groups: Zone 1 (super-intense: sides, belly, knees, pubic area), Zone 2 (intense: back, neck, underarms, feet) and Zone 3 (ticklerotic: most general erogenous zones). Of course, the sensitivity of your partner will determine the best place to stimulate. As again stated by Rueger (p. 166): "Your partner may have his or her own unique 'ticklenook' requiring special exploration." We suggest leaving this special ticklenook, your partner's best (worst?) spot, for last. Let him/her think that you've forgotten how ticklish his/her feet are. Sure you haven't, but there's no harm in letting him/her hope.

As for the type of touch to use, be lovingly evil, but also be considerate. Your partner's worst (best?) spot could be his/her ribs, which may be too sensitive for anything but the lightest scraping. His/her navel might be too sensitive for anything harder than a light licking before the touch becomes actually painful. This may be especially true right after orgasm, when sensitivity is often at its highest. Your object is to

20

cause helpless giggles, not winces of pain.

So how do you introduce the tickle (besides buying someone a copy of this book, that is)? There are two schools of thought. You can go in directly, making no apologies, or you can pretend to accidentally tickle while engaging in some other activity. We actually developed our mutual interest in tickling during a massage that turned into something else. The massaged partner got so tired of the "accidental" tickles that (after fair warning, of course) he seized the tickler, pinned her down, and gave her torso a good tickling. We haven't stopped since.

Massage

This is a favorite trick of tickling fans: to offer to give a massage and to sneak your tickles in while doing it. It's not your fault if you accidentally scrape a ticklish spot while you're massaging a sensitive foot, is it? It's not your fault if the person you're massaging is too sensitive, is it?

Begin by actually giving the massage. Make a mental note of any sensitive spots that might lead to a slight jump. After you're partner is thoroughly into it, alternate your kneading motions with tickling scrapes that you can still pretend are accidental. It'll become a game, with your partner looking up at your accusingly and you trying to look innocent. This can be a pleasurable activity for hours. If you prefer, after a while you can drop pretensions and begin a tickle wrestling match.

Something to be aware of is that some people lose their ticklishness when thoroughly relaxed. While this might submarine your tickling games, it means that you've brought your partner the pleasure of deep relaxation. That's probably worth the loss, especially since when (s)he comes back from the relaxed state (s)he'll be in a grateful mood and may be willing to indulge you a bit.

Tickling **Implements**

Tickling fans differ when it comes to the issue of using devices to tickle. Some purists prefer to only use fingertips to tease their lovers. Women in particular often have long fingernails that can be especially torturous on feet, underarms and torso. Used properly, they create ticklish shivers that can overwhelm the senses. Careful not to scratch or cut with those nails, though!

Such purists find that nothing can match the fingers for versatility and precision in stroking, kneading, and flicking. Others prefer to add other body parts such as hair or tongues for added effect. How about allowing your toes to get their own revenge by digging into your bound partner's ribs? Still

22

others prefer to introduce tickling toys into the act.

The stereotypical tickling toy is the feather. In tickle videos, cartoons, and cultural lore, the feather is symbolic of tickling. The hard truth is, though, that many people find that feathers just don't tickle. For these people the feather might provide a pleasing tingle or even an annoying itch, but no real tickles. Others swear by feathers, using soft ones on highly sensitive spots like between toes, and stiff ones on less ticklish spots. Try using the quill end instead of the feathery portion for variety, and see what that does. This is an area for experimentation.

Some ticklers report that melting ice can be used as an effective tickling agent. Even if it doesn't tickle, this can provide excellent skin sensitization. This is a favorite in many tickling videos, although the cynics claim that this is because it provides the actresses a break from real tickling. At the very least, melting ice can leave some moisture that a devilish tongue might have to lick up. Other foods or even wine can also be introduced to give an excuse to tongue-tickle.

Brushes of various sorts have been used by many ticklers, with great results. Artist brushes come in a variety of sizes and textures. The smallest and softest can torture the navel, ears, or between the toes. A larger one might brush under the arms or the feet. Care to paint pictures or write messages on your partner's belly or soles? You could, although you'll probably need to clean up after yourself with a nice soft scrub brush. Your partner won't resist, as long as (s)he is securely tied up. Again, experimentation with what is effective for you is crucial.

On a similar theme, fabrics and furs (please use FAKE FUR) have been used by some with great results. Again, experiment with textures and locations. You can find many such devices laying around your home (how about trying out that shaving brush on your partner's soles, or a pair of nylons slowly drawn across his/her underarms?)

Bondage positions

Bondage is one of the most popular sexual "variation" activities. Due to its popularity and the forces of capitalism, you can find commercially-made restraints relatively easily. If you're embarrassed to buy such devices or just prefer to be creative, simply make restraints from old ties or scarves. Be sure to use something that won't leave burns or bruises. If you use metal or plastic cuffs, get padded ones or place some material between skin and cuff. Make sure you have the key and that it works before locking!!! On a similar theme, be sure you can rapidly remove

24

whatever you use in case of cramping or emergency. Leave a knife or sharp scissors handy.

Any bondage position is fine for tickling, as long as it provides access to the vulnerable areas and prevents escape. Some of the favorite positions are:

1. Spread-eagled: your partner is tied down on the bed, stretched out, with all four limbs attached to the bed posts or legs at each corner. This provides easy access to the entire body. Turn your partner over and re-tie if you want access to his/her back. Some people find this more comfortable if a pillow is placed under the small of the back. That will also raise a ticklish belly a little closer to your fingertips, and give access to the sensitive area of the buttocks.

2. Hog-ties: your partner's arms and legs are tied together behind him. This also provides access to nearly every body part and also allows your partner to flop and roll, since (s)he is not secured to the bed.

3. Chair ties: your partner is tied to a chair. You can tie arms and legs to the chair's arms and legs, or tie your partners' arms over his/her head, or any combination.

4. Suspension: your partner is tied to the ceiling or door frame so that (s)he is stretched out. BE CAREFUL not to "hang" a person. Your objection is immobilization, not limb stretching. This will leave

the person completely vulnerable, except for the feet.
These you can simply pick up (one at a time) to give
the attention they deserve.

5. Mummy wraps: roll plastic wrap or a wet sheet
around your partner from ankle to shoulder. Those poor
little feet are just so irresistible!

6. Body bondage: your partner is restrained simply by
your weight and the way you're holding them (see
"tickle wrestling" below).

Sensory deprivation is often combined with
bondage. Many people report that when one sense is
temporarily cut off, they experience the other senses
(e.g., TOUCH) more intensely. Most of us tend to be
primarily visual responders, so something as simple as
a blindfold (commercially available as blindfolds or
"sleep shades," or make your own) can heighten your
partner's physical sensitivity tremendously. Blindfold
your partner, and then just watch for a minute.
Hoshikawa (1991) demonstrated that the expectation of a
tickle could be just as response-eliciting as the
actual tickle. After a little while, reach out with
the gentlest of touches and watch your partner react
like (s)he's received an electric shock. Do this a few
times. Let him/her wonder when you're going to touch
next, and where. Do this silently a few times. Tell
him/her that you're going to touch one place, then

touch another. Touch a few more times silently. Make sure you vary the places you touch. Move around a little so that your partner can hear your movement. (S)he'll be straining to hear, to get some clue of his/her fate. The uncertainty and anticipation can drive someone wild! This is often enough to get a reaction even from the "I'm not ticklish" people.

Tickle wrestling

As described by Russ Rueger (1981) in The Joy of Touch, tickle wrestling is a game where the two partners try to tickle each other at once. Of course, the loser is the one who gives up and surrenders first. The victor should be rewarded with some physical favor, usually agreed upon prior to the game. For some extra spice, try negotiating the favor when one partner is at the breaking point. You'll be surprised what sorts of offers you hear, or what you find yourself offering when you're at your partner's mercy. The only problem is: won't you still be willing to promise all that and more if asked "what's it worth to you to have me stop" after five **more** minutes of tickling? Just pray that your partner doesn't think of that when she has you right where she wants you.

Don't be overconfident when it comes to tickle wrestling, guys. Rueger correctly warns that women often have a lighter and softer touch and thus make more effective ticklers. An article in <u>Mademoiselle</u> magazine authored by Farrel reached the same conclusion.

There are many "tickle holds" that are nearly impossible to break unless there is a great strength difference between partners. Even if a great strength difference exists prior to the "match," the stress of the struggle can be a great equalizer. Some holds to try:

1. If one partner can scissor the other's foot between his/her calves, that leaves a helpless foot available for tickling.

2. Laying on a partner's arm and holding his/her other arm under your partner's head with one hand leaves you with a free hand and a whole torso to tickle and tease to your heart's content (this position is called "Tickletorture" by Rueger).

3. If you can manage to trap both of your partner's wrists in one of your hands, hold them over his/her head. Wrap up one or both of his/her legs with yours. This will achieve the same effect as hold # 2.

4. Laying on a partner's back while (s) is face down is a good bet for being able to tease the upper torso with little resistance.

5. The "tickle hug" is great if your partner's ribs are more ticklish than yours. Simply hug your partner

and drop down so that you are laying down with you on top and his/her back on the bed. Then extend your fingers a little farther so that you and your partner are in a nice tight hug. Gently dig into those vulnerable ribs. Even though your partner's hands are completely free, (s)he will be unlikely to reach your hands and will be forced to surrender.

Any one of these holds is a virtually sure win. Make sure to negotiate for something fun, you've earned it. Your partner will be only too happy to oblige. If not, check back with him after another minute or two of intensive tickling.

Verbal and physical teasing

What separates a masterful tickler from an amateur is not so much the actual tickling as the absence of tickling. Anyone can tickle, but it takes a person with imagination and sensitivity to know when not to tickle and therefore how to build tension. Fingertips wiggling inches over exposed underarms can be more exciting than the actual tickles, teasing the ticklee into a frenzy of anticipation. Giving breaks that let the ticklee relax and just begin to feel safe before starting again can also be great for building tension.

For building tension, though, nothing can match a good verbal teasing. The teasing can come before, during, or after the tickling. Most cultures seem to

29

have some characteristic nonsense sound that comes along with tickling. In Japan it is a "cotyo cotyo" sound. In the United States it is "koochie koochie koo" or a game of "this little piggy." In Greece, it is a "kileek kileek" sound (and, according to Greek folklore, only jealous people are ticklish). In Germany, it is a "kitz kitz" sound. These sounds accompany the actual tickling and heighten the sensations by highlighting the person's helplessness.

After-tickling teasing usually takes the form of question asking. Use a teasing tone of voice and coo things like:

1. "Did you like that?"
2. "Aw, did that tickle?"
3. "You're really ticklish, aren't you?"
4. "Ready for more?"
5. "Want me to let you go? I'm not going to!"

For really driving your partner crazy, though, nothing can beat pre-tickling teasing. In the movie Summer Lovers, there's a fine example. Daryl Hannah's character has her boyfriend tied up. She verbally teases him, finally culminating with a devilish look in her eye and the words, "Are you afraid I might tickle you? Because I might...!" She then begins tickling his ribs and underarms. Before he's even touched, however, her partner begins begging "No, not that! No!

No!" and then dissolves into helpless giggles. Ever notice how people begin to laugh before that last little piggy goes all the way home? Such verbal teasing lets your partner anticipate (dread?) what's coming, and realize his/her helplessness to prevent it. Examples of such teases include:

1. "Here it comes."
2. "Ready?"
3. "What's the matter? Why so nervous?"
4. "Can't stop me, can you?"
5. "Where are you the most ticklish? I think I can find out if you don't want to tell me."
6. "What's it worth to you for me not to tickle you?"
7. "Feeling ticklish today?"
8. "If you want more, just laugh and squirm!"

Feel free to experiment with all sorts of ways to tickle and tease. This is supposed to be playful and fun. This is not a time to be self-conscious, but to allow yourselves to laugh and play together the way lovers are supposed to. You remember, the way you did when you were first falling in love.

Chapter 3: Favorite Tickling Games

This is our favorite chapter to write. Here we
describe some of the scenarios we and other ticklers
have found conducive to creating the proper mood, not
to mention just plain fun. Some of the themes of these
tickling games are included in our tickling fiction
section. Most require no more equipment than a good
imagination.

While the themes of these various games are very
different, they all share one thing in common: they
provide a plausible means of introducing tickling into
an interaction. They build the tension of the
"victim," as (s)he wonders when the "action" will
begin, and just how the tickling will be introduced.
They create a power situation, with one of the partners
adopting the role of victim, or "resister" if you
prefer. The resister is testing his/her willpower,
seeing how long (s)he can prolong the fun. The tickler
is attempting to break down the resister, but is also
careful to make sure not to end the action too quickly
by taking too early advantage of any weaknesses. Be
sure to have a running dialogue with the victim.
Verbal teasing is every bit as important to the
excitation of both partners as the actual tickles.

When playing any of these games, remember that
THEY ARE GAMES. Games have rules. The first and

32

foremost rule for these games is respect for the safeword. On a related theme, games are consensual. Nonconsensual tickling, or tickling that passes one's limit, is cruel (advice columnist Dear Abby has branded nonconsensual tickling a form of abuse in several columns), and counterproductive in the end. Don't forget what a helpless position your partner is adopting as an expression of trust in you. If you violate that trust, that's one partner who will never play with you again. Trust in other areas might suffer, too.

The second rule: HAVE FUN.

Fantasy Games for You and Your Partner

Here are a few of our favorite role-playing games. They also provide much of the material for the plots (such as they sometimes are) of the fetish magazine and video market (see resource chapter). In no particular order, they are:

1. Revenge is a favorite theme of tickle fantasy writers and fetish video makers. One person has committed some grievous wrong to another, and the wronged party exacts revenge by making the other person helpless and tickle-torturing them. This type of game is very high in dialogue, as confessions, apologies, and promises to never do it again are tortured from the victim. Lots of nasty teasing is called for as well.

Revenge games can spring from pure fantasy ("I saw the way you looked at her and now you're gonna get it!") to real-life events ("You'll never bounce another check again!"). The important thing, though, is to make sure that the game is pleasurable for both partners. This is not a game to play when angry, with thinly disguised torture being inflicted in the name of sexual play. Don't imagine that your partner is your obnoxious boss and forget that you are actually with the person you love. Obviously, don't use this game to exact revenge for something that you really are angry about or this will be the last time your partner ever agrees to play with you.

2. The _interrogation_ is the next most popular theme for fantasy writers and players. In this scenario, the job of the tickler is to force the ticklee to reveal some secret information. Again, this can be as elaborate or as simple as you care to make it. During one of the Howard Stern television program on the Entertainment Network (E!), Howard attempted to tickle a secret word out of three willing and bound victims. All lasted the full two and one half minute time limit without revealing the secret word (and thus earned a $192 prize). In between women, Howard took phone calls from listeners who confessed to being enormously sexually aroused. Howard confessed to being aroused

34

during the taping and openly wondered whether he might be a "tickle fetishist." This was the third (but not the last) time that Howard had featured bound tickling of women on his program, as well as some non-bound tickling of his female guests. While tickling fans appreciated the exposure for their turn-on, perhaps to make it more mainstream so that it will be dealt with more openly and seriously, discussions on the computer networks (see Chapter 4) suggested that some felt that the ticking was done too much in a side-show fashion. Many felt their turn-on had been ridiculed. We liked it.

The themes can be much more elaborate than Howard's "game show," however. For example, one partner can play a captured spy while the other plays an interrogator. A member of a rival organization may have been caught attempting espionage and must be forced to betray his/her secrets (see the tickling fiction section). A favorite television or movie character has been caught by a villain and is being grilled for information. Remember, this is fantasy. You can be anyone you desire. How about a hypnotist combining his/her skills with tickling, or just the suggestion of it?

3. Negotiation is a fantasy game where the partners pretend to be on opposite sides of a bargaining table,

conducting hard-nosed negotiations. Somehow the information that one party is terribly ticklish is dropped or discovered. The other party takes advantage of this fact to make the negotiations turn his/her way.

4. Mugging is a game where one partner tries to take something (e.g., a $20 bill) from the other partner. The game might begin with one partner asking the other for a loan, a request which is refused. The turned down party is persistent and eventually touches a ticklish spot while nagging. The "discovered" vulnerability is exploited, as the tickling partner "realizes" the power they have over the stingy one. The game lasts until the $20 is given away, no repayment necessary.

5. Employment games involve tickling between bosses and employees. Perhaps an employee has been caught stealing. The employee can either be fired or accept the tickling punishment.

Another variation is an obnoxious boss that has to be taught a lesson. You can make this very elaborate: pretend that you've kidnapped the boss and are in a remote location where no one can hear him/her scream. (S)he has to promise to mend his/her ways or the information about his/her vulnerability will be leaked, or perhaps even a videotape distributed. This game, like the others, is very heavy on dialogue.

6. If you play <u>School</u>, you can keep a student after
school to reprimand him/her for cheating on a test.
The student may be properly repentant and willing to do
anything you want just so that you won't fail him/her
or call his/her parents. It's up to you to take what
you can get. Or, the student might be unwilling to
admit that (s)he did anything wrong. With a little
tickling in just the right places, you might be able to
elicit an apology and perhaps an extra-credit
assignment.

You can also come at this from another
perspective. A student who needs an "A" that (s)he
doesn't really deserve in order to stay on the
cheerleading/football team can try to persuade his/her
teacher to pass him/her, either by offering a favor
("I'll let you...") or by refusing to let the teacher
up from some torturous tickle-hold until (s)he agrees
to raise the grade.

7. <u>Historical themes</u> are popular with tickling fans.
The bound partner might be a woman being interrogated
as a witch at the Salem trials, or perhaps a prisoner
of the Spanish Inquisition. Mata Hari might be in the
mood to tickle some information from her male victim.
In a tribute to the Russian practice, perhaps Catherine
the Great would bring in a member of the Ticklers
religious order to service her, or perhaps would be

captured against her will by the sect. Perhaps Catherine might be in the mood to do the tickling herself (see Great Catherine in the movies section). A particularly stern monastic order might require a penance of tickling for some major (or minor, for that matter) offense. Some partners like to really get into this, involving costumes and period music. You can make it as elaborate or simple as you see fit. The real key is, of course, imagination.

8. Super-hero oriented fantasies are great for the young at heart. What if Wonder Woman found herself tied up with her own magic lasso? Or what if she decided to interrogate a super-villain after completing her hog-tie? Did Batman have a feather in his utility belt? How would Catwoman have reacted to that? Was kryptonite really Superman's only weakness? You get the idea.

9. Discovery games involve one partner "discovering" that the other is ticklish and deciding to have a little fun. In this, it is similar to some of the other games we've described. What changes is the context. Here's where you get to show your creativity. Perhaps a shoe salesperson "accidentally" discovers a pair of ticklish feet just around closing time. Perhaps a doctor's physical examination is complicated by the "sensitivity" of his patient. In the movie

Dirty Dancing, Patrick Swayze, much to his annoyance, discovers the ticklishness of Jennifer Grey's underarms while teaching her to dance. No tickler would have allowed this opportunity to go by without further exploration. In Hivnor's drama, The Ticklish Acrobat, a specialist is called in to see if he can eliminate ticklishness in a young woman because just such accidental tickles keep occurring and are potentially life-threatening due to the nature of her work.

10. In humility games, the object is for one partner to act the role of the stereotypical arrogant, stuck-up, self-styled "stud" or "babe." Perhaps the tickled individual can play the role of a martial arts expert or bodybuilder who thinks that (s)he is invulnerable to ANY type of attack. The individual must be thoroughly obnoxious, so that (s)he can be taken down a peg or two or ten. Your object is to teach a little humility. Take the conceited person and turn him/her into a sex slave with your skilled fingertips. This game calls for heavy verbal teasing to really highlight the helpless role of the "victim."

Acting out Fantasies in the Real World

Sometimes real world experiences are disappointing compared to fantasies. They just can't live up to the perfection that the mind's eye can create. Other times, though, fantasy just can't compare to what the real world can deliver. While tickling occasions often arise spontaneously, the odds of a good experience can be increased with a little planning.

Both partners don't necessarily have to plan together, incidentally - it's also nice to set up a "surprise" for your partner. A catch phrase is helpful to signal the beginning of a fantasy scene, so that your partner has some idea of where you're coming from. Use dialogue to clarify your role and your partner's role in the scene, and you haven't had to ruin any of the mood by explaining ("Okay, so I'm the bad girl, and you're the headmaster, right, and you have to punish me for cheating on the test by tickling me. Okay? Now we start.")

Public Tickles

A great way to tease your partner is to tickle him or her in public. No one else will know that you're engaging in foreplay, but you will. Tickle your lover while you're laying together on the beach or in the park. Funny how many people will be covertly watching, isn't it? Is it possible that maybe some of these people are getting very turned on and trying to hide it? What if you whispered a threat to your partner to invite these on-lookers to join in? You both know it probably wouldn't be too difficult to convince one of those hazy-eyed voyeurs to join in.

You can be very creative with public tickles. At dinner, pretend to be playing footsie and covertly pick up your partner's foot under the table and hold it in your lap between your knees. It will be very difficult for him/her to carry on a proper conversation if you tease their tender skin just when they're trying to make a point or even to just listen attentively. Better yet, do this in a restaurant or at a dinner party where an outburst of giggling would be very inappropriate. Be careful, though, especially if you're ticklish, too - who knows what you'll get when you get home, or the next time YOU'RE in a socially and/or physically sensitive situation!

Threesomes and Moresomes

A very popular fantasy for couples to act out is a group tickling scene. While such a scene can evolve into actual sex, this is not necessary. Sometimes the tickling is the aim, and the sex comes later, in private, with both partners too turned on to breathe properly. In this type of fantasy, there are several possibilities, but here are a few suggestions:

1. Both partners tickle another individual.

2. One of the partners is tickled by another while the second partner watches or even gives directions.

3. One of the partners is "gang-tickled" by the partner and an assistant.

41

4. Lovers take turns being tickled by, and tickling, another individual in every combination and permutation you can think of.

The key to this game, is, of course, to find the right third and/or fourth (or more). A likely candidate will probably be:

1. A close friend of both partners (someone not liked or trusted by either half of the couple is probably not a good choice since trust and genuine affection is very important to the mood).

2. Someone who is not too conservative and has a good sense of humor.

3. Someone who is ticklish (but you didn't need to be told that).

Your friend's personality will already be known to you, so the real issue here may be assessing ticklishness and willingness to participate. This can be done in several ways:

1. Bring up tickling in a conversation by describing an imaginary (or real) tickle on television or in real life.

2. Watch one of the movies listed in our tickling movies chapter with him or her. See how (s)he responds to a discussion of the scene.

3. Listen to Carly Simon's "Are you ticklish?" song from the Playing Possum CD (the song is about

emotional, rather than physical, sensitivity). Ask if
(s)he is ticklish.

4. If you're especially bold, try to give a little
tickle once the information has been dropped. No sense
in not being straight forward.

5. Try "The Tickler" game discussed in the next
chapter. Step up the games gradually or introduce the
idea all at once, based upon the responses you're
getting.

Deviously enough, you don't even always have to
tell the third member of your party what (s)he is
involved in. A playful friend might be engaged in a
tickling match in sight of your partner. This is a
nice "show" for one partner to give to the other. You
are both aware of the purpose behind the action, and
there is that feeling of an inside joke to make you
feel even more intimate with each other. For "closet
exhibitionists" (admittedly a paradox if not an
oxymoron), it can be intensely exciting to engage in a
very public tickling match. This type of play is not
recommended, however, for people who are jealous of
others coming into physical contact with their partner.
As with everything else, know your partner and the
prospective other before you try this one.

Videotape roulette

A game that we've derived much pleasure from is

called videotape roulette. In this game, one partner is bound to the bed. The television and VCR are oriented so that the bound person has full view of the screen. The VCR is loaded with a tickling fetish video tape (see Chapter 4, Resources for Ticklers), and the VCR remote is in the hands of the unbound partner.

The bound person verbally controls the remote, telling the unbound partner to either:

1. "fast forward"

2. "rewind"

3. "play"

When the tape plays, the bound partner experiences whatever is showing on the screen for a period of one minute. Then (s)he gets to give an instruction to move the tape again. If (s)he is lucky, the tape stops at a point where little tickling is going on, or at least on a spot that (s)he can handle. If unlucky, well, it's his/her own fault. After all, (s)he told you to stop there! With a little experience with a particular tape, a shrewd player will try to measure time (don't use the scan feature when moving the tape!) so that it stops at a relatively safe position. You can block this strategy by changing tapes often.

Set up your own rules for penalties/rewards for the use of the safeword while playing this game. We find that favors of escalating magnitude for higher

44

numbers of minutes endured without using the safeword is satisfying to us both. The bound partner may get somewhat competitive, playing to beat last time's total minutes endured.

Be Careful of Clubs and Personals!!!

Sometimes D & S clubs advertise tickling parties for like-minded people to get together. You can also find tickling personals in personals columns or on computer bulletin boards. As we have warned throughout, BE CAREFUL!!! Any time you are entering into a situation where bondage or any control/power situation might be an issue, make sure you know your partner first. Even though tickling may seem playful, and your potential partner may talk the talk and walk the walk, you are still putting yourself in a highly vulnerable position or putting someone else in that situation. What's to stop that person from later claiming that the game was not consensual? A couple of bruises on that person's wrists will be more persuasive than your denials. You need to know that you are with someone who has your pleasure in mind as well as his/her own, someone who will respect the safeword and your limits. You can easily find yourself in an abusive situation, or in a different sort of "ticklish situation" than the one you've fantasized about if you're not careful.

On a less serious note, sometimes clubs advertise theme evenings but none of the attendees seem to know about it (we've had this experience twice). Do your homework and make sure a scheduled event isn't just on paper. It'll save you making a trip to a sleazy neighborhood for an event you have no interest in (it's a wide world, with LOTS of different interests), or finding out that nobody really pays attention to the written schedules anyway.

The Reluctant Partner

As we described earlier, some people have a real dislike of being tickled. These games may help you to introduce tickling to a reluctant partner, but they also may not. You must always bear in mind that tickling is a consensual activity. If your partner truly hates to be tickled and is not willing to "desensitize" through trusting play, there is little you can do. Someone who wishes to be tickled, rather than to do the tickling, may have an easier time of it, but not necessarily. Simply springing the game on your partner is to run a risk. Your partner may react very badly, either not taking you seriously (ouch!) or even displaying some degree of disgust or shock (double ouch!). You can also anger a person if they have made their feelings on the matter quite clear already.

Unfortunately, some couples go through life with

one partner desiring to experiment with sexual variations and the other partner unwilling to try. Your partner may have had a very strict upbringing regarding what is "proper," and such conditioning can be very difficult to undo (see, for example, discussions by Masters and Johnson of this dilemma). All you can do is be as open and communicative with your partner as possible, and make every attempt to demonstrate how much such activities excite you. Give your lover time, and their love for you may help to dispel their fears.

This is no different than any other area of sexual disagreement. If your partner is unable or unwilling to provide you with what you want, you may have to be content with fantasy. Your only other recourse is to reevaluate the relationship, and we would hope it wouldn't come to that.

Chapter 4:   Resources for Ticklers

For communicating with other ticklers at any moment of the day or night, the modern computer age is now accommodating us. Compuserve's Human Sexuality forum (Go Hsx 200) has a Foot and Tickling Fun bulletin board (Section 13). The internet features its alt.sex.fetish.tickling newsgroup. Internet's alt.sex.fetish.feet also has its share of tickling fans.

Both boards feature messages that you can read and post, library stories (fiction and nonfiction) and general resource sharing (e.g., tips for movies/TV shows during that week that will feature a tickling scene, and hopefully wonderful reviews of this book). Compuserve even has weekly conferences where people get together to discuss their favorite fun. In fact, we learned of the existence of the toy described in our next section from a telecomputer message, and received many of the tips for our movie scene chapter from there.

"The Tickler"

Eldorado produces a game called "The Tickler". The game comes with a playing board and two feathers (each different in size and texture). The object of this game is to make move your piece all the way around the game board. Spots on the game board are marked with different instructions to tickle or to receive a tickle from your partner on a particular body spot in a particular fashion. There are rewards and penalties for reactions.

This game is most competitive when played by partners who are roughly equal in ticklishness. You need not be ticklish in the same places, the board instructs you to stimulate different areas. Sooner or later you'll hit your partner's weak spot. To spice up the game, you might even play for stakes. Perhaps the winner might earn an extra reward, or the loser some punishment, just to make the game even more interesting than it already is.

The game need not be played that way, of course, and competition is only appropriate at particular times. Some games are just for the fun of the moment. Or are they? The Tickler might be used as a tool to introduce the topic. Someone who wants to incite a partner into tickling might suggest a game, with an eye to showing just how exciting it can be.

The game can also be used to put on a show for your partner (see "threesomes and moresomes" from the previous chapter). You might play a third party, with your partner watching on (and probably blinking only rarely and breathing erratically). All of you can play at once, and the team concept introduces even more

possibilities. How about a nice round robin
tournament? The address for the producer of the game
is Eldorado, Boulder, Colorado 80301. We obtained our
copy from Scarlet's in Laguna Beach, California.

Books, magazines, and journals

A classic, but difficult to find, piece of
Victorian erotica was <u>A Man with a Maid</u>. We have seen
the title listed as "out of press" by both Grovye Press
and Ballantine Books, but don't know if it's the same
story anyway. Following the theme of much D & S
erotica, the woman begins as resisting the advances of
her male dominant, only to be taken against her will
and seduced by the new experiences. In this case, the
tool of domination was the feather. The female
submissive was so taken by the experiences that she
felt a need to act out the role of dominant by tickling
other unconsenting women along with her dom.

A book we enjoyed immensely was Dr. Russ Rueger's
<u>The Joy of Touch</u>. This book is practically unique in
that includes a couple of pages devoted exclusively to
sexual tickling, pages that would do any tickling
enthusiast proud (p. 166):

"But when a lover does it, aggression merges with
affection, which gives tickling its unique creative
power..."

We must caution, however, that we do not feel that Rueger emphasized consent nearly enough. Describing using tickling to overcome orgasmic difficulty, Rueger writes (p. 166):

"Sustained tickling can literally drive someone out of his mind, thus loosening its tenacious grip on the body."

Later (p. 168) we find:

"Practically speaking, tickletorture can only be done male to female. . . .It can be most useful with women who are uptight about climaxing. In most tickle play, the female can use countermeasures. She can tickle back, bounce off the bed, grab the guy's hands, or just leave. She can't do any of that with tickletorture. You can literally drive her out of her senses."

As we've stated before, this could be well be one partner who will never agree to play with you again. Despite this one caution, we really loved <u>The Joy of Touch</u>, and for more than just the tickling chapter. It's really well-written book, one of our favorites.

For the dramatically minded, there is Hivnor's

play, <u>The Ticklish Acrobat</u>. The relation of ticklishness to sexual experience is explored in this narrative as well (p. 70):

"Zanelli: You know, back in the States we know a little bit about curing hiccups and ticklishness and things like that. . . .I mean it's <u>deep</u>. It has something to do with the sex set-up. . . .I'd marry her first-that'd cure the ticklishness."

In the course of the play, Zanelli proves his theory correct (p. 124):

"Father Zugo: Yes, Joe convinced me. He cured my daughter of the tickles. However, after that she began to get sick in the morning..."

The folk wisdom that ticklishness fades in women with sexual experience was also mentioned by Orchnik (1958). Orchnik took an additional, somewhat controversial step when he also claimed to confirm some folk wisdom regarding the damaging effects of the prolonged tickling of children. Orchnik believed that children who had suffered prolonged tickling as children were likely to develop stuttering. He further referenced a case reported by famed psychoanalyst Helene Deutsch of a woman who would collapse to the floor when tickled as a result of early trauma with prolonged tickling. It is important to note, however, that nearly forty years later Orchnik's observations have not yet been confirmed. No major theory of psychopathology blames childhood tickling for any adult pathology, except perhaps a dislike of being tickled. Another psychoanalyst, Phillips (1993), in fact, recently suggested that adult tickling of children served a purpose in their psychological development. It helps children to distinguish real from imaginary threats: Mommy isn't <u>really</u> going to "get" me, she's just going to tickle me. The key, as in adult/adult tickling, seems to be to not let it get out of hand. Weisberg (1976) reported that as children aged, in fact, they preferred tickling to cuddling forms of physical contact.

Tickling was related to psychotherapy by one more theorist, with unfortunate results. In the 1970s, a form of "psychotherapy" known as Z Process (also known as Rage Reduction or Attachment Therapy, see books authored in the 1970s by Dr. Robert Zaslow) was practiced. Z Process involved having several people hold a client motionless while a "therapist" asked questions. If unsatisfied with the client's answer, the therapist would tickle the client's ribs to elicit a rage reaction. Elvis Presley and Mary Tyler Moore demonstrated this technique on a young girl with autism in a film entitled A Change of Habit. This practice was never really popular, but fell even farther from favor when a client suffered kidney damage as a result of treatment (Meyers, Landis, & Hayes, 1988). Again, in all fairness, the physical stimulation probably escalated above mere tickling here. Your chances of causing such tissue damage by tickling are probably minimal unless you get carried away and use FAR too much force.

For the academically minded, there are many such discussions of tickling and ticklishness that can give additional information. While the journal articles tend to be clinical, and the books contain only fleeting references to tickling, they can still be informative. Check our reference section for further suggestions.

Fetish Magazines and Videos

For the hardcore tickler, of course, nothing but material specifically aimed at their favorite pass-time will do. Fortunately, such materials are now readily available in magazine and video format.

Each company that we will list here seems to have its own style, its own particular niche in the market. Individual tastes vary, and so will the material you seek out. Do you want a plot, or just lots and lots of tickling? Is the attractiveness of the actors and actresses more important than their actual ticklishness? Do you care if plots are plausible? Do you prefer a lot of dialogue, or do you just want action? All of these factors will help you to decide on a company and their products.

On the video front, our hands-down favorite video company is Harmony Productions. Their tapes offer us what we appreciate most: good running dialogue between the performers, as well as genuinely good action.

Harmony Concepts
P.O. Box 69976
Los Angeles, CA 90069

California Star/Direct has a series of Tied and Tickled tapes, some of which we have also enjoyed. While we have enjoyed their tapes that emphasize some communication between performers, they also have a number of tapes with a "monster" or villain theme where dialogue is at a minimum. According to the folk-lore of tickle devotees, Cal Star's models tend to be pulled from the general X-Rated film pool of performers. Cal Star also has "Tied and Tickled Classics" highlight tapes that can help you to choose tapes that suit your tastes.

California Star/Direct
641 West Ave. J.
Suite 413
Lancaster, CA 93534

Another company that is becoming a hit among ticklers is TJ Productions: (201) 288-1266. This company creates tickling tapes, and emphasizes their reality. All tickling and reactions are REAL (according to the producers who also happen to be tickling aficionados). We've enjoyed their products immensely.

On-line you can also hook up with organizations like the World Wide Tickle club and see advertisements/hear reviews for videos by Pam and Solefully yours, both of which have been highly recommended. We don't have personal knowledge, but are willing to take other's words for it. New people and companies go on-line all the time. Get there!

Other companies exist to serve this niche market; we suggest hitting the computer bulletin boards for suggestions for companies that specialize in YOUR particular interest in tickling. If you're not computer literate, magazines like Leg Show and Fetish Times feature classifieds that may help. Check those newsstands! Tickling is becoming more and more popular all the time!!!

Chapter 5: Favorite Tickling Movie Scenes

While there are countless specialized tickling videos available for purchase (see our resource list), the quality of these is highly variable. Some are, let's be honest, just plain awful (see descriptions of exceptions in resource list). They have lousy acting, little or no real tickling, and make no sense. They generally show minutes of senseless fake tickling with performers who are obviously not ticklish, ignoring the greater psychology involved.

In contrast, scenes in mainstream movies, although very difficult to find and seconds (as opposed to minutes) in length, tend to be of higher quality and are prized by collectors. The following list has been compiled from suggestions given by collectors on computer bulletin boards.

Tickling scenes in movies are notorious for being brief and for fading out during the action. It's as though the directors don't know exactly what to do with it, and find tickling embarrassing In the recent film version of Exit to Eden, for example, despite the D & S theme of the movie, we see only one brief tickle scene. There was no laughter, and the woman walked away from her "bondage" in response to a loudspeaker announcement. When used at all, tickling is used to effectively convey sensual playfulness (see for example, <u>A Change of Seasons</u>, <u>A Bunny's Tale</u>, <u>Forever Young</u>, <u>Mind Over Murder</u> or <u>The World's Oldest Living Bridesmaid</u>).

What follows is a partial list, since the only way to find out what's out there is to watch movies and compare notes with other interested parties. Some of the movies that are almost always mentioned in any such discussion are listed here:

1. <u>A CHANGE OF SEASONS</u>: In this classic tickling scene, Michael Brandon tickles Shirley Maclaine's ribs and "forces" her to play a game of "trust me," which involves leaving one's self vulnerable to a tickling. Very good laughing and dialogue, and a long scene for the genre.

2. <u>NORTH TO ALASKA</u>: Widely regarded as another classic, Stewart Granger tickles the female star's stockinged foot to make her laugh in order to make John Wayne jealous.

3. <u>THE BROTHERS KARAMAZOV</u>: Lee J. Cobb ties and tickles Maria Schell's bare feet with a feather in this adaptation of the Russian literary classic that is also a classic among ticklers.

4. <u>HOUDINI</u>: Tony Curtis tickles Janet Leigh's feet as they stick out of the "saw a lady in half" box. Such tickling is common with this particular magic act and can usually be found with any "saw the person half"

performance. Mark Wilson, in particular, is known for including tickling as part of this illusion.

5. HE KNOWS YOU'RE ALONE: A teasing woman is trapped in a half-closed window and rib tickled by her lover. He tickles until she agrees to have sex on the kitchen table, then tickles her some more for good measure.

6. MICKI AND MAUDE: Dudley Moore tickles Amy Irving's ribs in two different scenes. In the first Dudley accidentally touches Amy's ticklish spot, leading her to confess that she's very ticklish. Later, he tickles her ribs during a playful fight.

7. FOREVER YOUNG: Mel Gibson tickles his fiancee in a playful scene known for its teasing dialogue (he tickles her as a rehearsal for torture she might receive if he tells her a particular secret). As soon as Mel mentions "the most painful kind of torture," his fiancee realizes her plight and threatens to scream. The scene fades out on the tickling as she begs him not to tickle her knees.

8. THE REAL McCOY: Kim Bassinger is playfully tickled on her ribs by a young boy she has been teasing, as she begs him not to. The familiar fade-out. Alicia Silverstone is also rib-tickled by some children in The Babysitter, and the family father gets in a rib-tickle of his own.

9. BETWEEN FRIENDS: Carol Burnett gets her bare feet

tickled by an admitted foot fetishist. She explodes in
laughter and admits that she likes it when he gives her
a quick break. Fade out on the scene, which is long
for the genre.

10. SPYS: Donald Sutherland tickles the feet (not
shown, under covers) of a young woman. Excellent
laughter and teasing.

11. BOUND FOR GLORY: David Carradine tickles his
wife's ribs in a playful "blackmail" scenario that many
ticklers find irresistible (see also Stripes and
Falling from Grace for this type of "blackmail"
scenario).

12. WHERE THE WOMEN GO: Young woman is playfully rib-
tickled by her boyfriend.

13. I LIKE THE GIRLS WHO DO: A woman is rib-tickled
to force her to give up an item in her possession. A
favorite of collectors.

14. BAD MEDICINE: Steve Guttenberg tickles Julie
Harris' feet. Wonderful laughing, but all action is
invisible because the couple are under the covers.

15. SUMMER LOVERS: Daryl Hannah ties and tickles her
boyfriend's ribs, after first verbally teasing him (see
description in an earlier chapter).

16. SIRENS: Considered a classic by collectors, the
action centers around Elle MacPhearson. In three
different scenes, she discusses or actually delivers

tickles to other women in the movie. This is considered by collectors to be one of the most erotic demonstrations of the sensuality of tickling in mainstream film.

17. O'HARA'S WIFE: Ed Asner and Mariette Hartley have a rib-tickling fight. Both laugh hysterically, but Mariette loses.

18. UP THE SAND-BOX: Barbara Streisand tickles her husband while holding his feet for sit-ups. This leads to more playful interactions, but no further tickling.

19. SECOND THOUGHTS: Lucie Arnaz and her boyfriend have a tickling fight (invisible, under covers). She is forced to yell, "I give! I give!"

20. PERSONAL BEST: Marielle Hemingway and her lesbian lover have a discussion of tickling while stroking each other.

21. ROBOCOP 2: In a flashback, Robo briefly tickles his wife's bare foot. She appears to have been teasing him with her feet, and reacts extremely strongly to the tickle.

22. DIRTY DANCING: Patrick Swayze tickles Jennifer Gray under the arms twice while teaching her to dance. On the third pass she does not react.

23. MOON OVER PARADOR: Richard Dreyfuss has his feet tickled by his lover.

24. YOU CAN'T STOP THE MUSIC: Valerie Perrine tickles

Bruce Jenner's feet after playing "this little piggy."
Before she tickles, Bruce admits that he's ticklish.

25. THE LAST SONG: Linda Carter and her daughter have
a rib-tickling fight. Linda gives excellent pre-
tickling physical and verbal teases.

26. THE PIANO: Holly Hunter's daughter tickles her
under the arms during a tickling fight.

27. YENTL: Barbara Streisand has her ribs tickled by
Many Patinkin, who is trying to force her to admit that
she is wrong on a point.

28. JUST ONE OF THE GUYS: A woman (dressed as a man)
is briefly tickled on the stomach by another woman.

29. HOPE AND GLORY: Husband tickles his wife's ribs.

30. CRAZY FROM THE HEART: Christine Lahti has her
stockinged feet tickled by Ruben Blades. This scene is
a favorite of both tickling and foot fans for its views
of Christine's wiggling soles and her laughter.

31. LIKE MOM, LIKE ME: Young Kristy McNichol is rib
tickled by boyfriend. Scene fades out on tickle.

32. THE BABE: John Goodman gets ribs tickled by
girlfriend.

33. AN UNMARRIED WOMAN: Jill Clayburgh gets her legs
tickled by her boyfriend. This turns more sexual and
the scene fades out.

34. GHOULIES: Woman gets her ribs tickled by
boyfriend.

35. MIND OVER MURDER: Deborah Rafkin gets tickled in two scenes. First her ears are tickled with a kiss. Later her foot is briefly tickled in the same way.

36. DESPERATELY SEEKING SUSAN: Madonna briefly tickles the foot of a sleeping boyfriend.

37. OVERBOARD: Goldie Hawn gets her ribs gang-tickled by a group of children. The scene fades out on the tickling and Goldie's helpless laughter.

38. THE WOMEN'S ROOM: Lee Remick is rib-tickled by Gregory Harrison and her two sons. The scene fades out on the tickling.

39. THE OWL AND THE PUSSYCAT: Barbara Streisand gets a brief tickle on the sole of her foot (Barbara's third appearance on our list).

40. THE BLUE LAGOON: Brooke Shields and Christopher Atkins have a brief rib-tickling fight. She loses.

41. POLTERGEIST: JoBeth Williams gets her ribs tickled in two different scenes. JoBeth also got a quick rib-tickle in POLTERGEIST 2.

42. A KING IN NEW YORK: In a talking role, Charlie Chaplin holds and briefly tickles the bare foot of a young woman.

43. CARMEN JONES: Harry Belafonte tickles a woman's feet by blowing on them.

44. BONNIE AND CLYDE: THE TRUE STORY: Bonnie and Clyde take turns tickling the toes of a woman whose

foot is in a cast. This TV movie is prized among ticklers for the woman's reactions and pleading.

45. WORLD'S OLDEST LIVING BRIDESMAID: Donna Mills gets her ribs tickled by her boyfriend, who pretends not to know that she is ticklish.

46. A BUNNY'S TALE: Kirstie Alley gets her torso tickled by her husband. The scene fades out on the tickling.

47. TARZAN OF THE APES: Johnny Weismuller tickles Maureen O'Sullivan's foot. The 1959 remake also features such a scene.

48. THE PRIZE PULITZER: Chynna Phillips' husband tickles her feet briefly.

49. ENORMOUS CHANGES (AT THE LAST MINUTE): Ellen Barkin is tickled on the ribs by her husband.

50. COME TO THE STABLE: Hugh Marlowe tickles Dorothy Patrick's ribs.

51. FALLING FROM GRACE: John Mellencamp tickles Marielle Hemingway's ribs to "force" her to tell him that she loves him.

52. STRIPES: Bill Murray tickles P.J. Soles with a variety of kitchen implements to "force" a similar confession.

53. POINT OF NO RETURN: Bridgette Fonda gets her foot briefly tickled by a kiss. See Mind Over Murder, Chain of Desire and Making Mr. Right for similar scenes.

54. GREAT CATHERINE: Catherine the Great ties and tickles Peter O'Toole.

55. BALL OF FIRE: A male villain is torso-tickled with a feather to force him to divulge information.

56. ELVIS AND THE BEAUTY QUEEN: Stephanie Zimblast gets her feet briefly tickled by her female co-star.

57. NO WAY TO TREAT A LADY: Rod Steiger tickles the ribs of a woman before strangling her. This is a long scene for the genre with excellent laughter, marred by the context.

58. BABY DOLL: Movie based on Tennessee Williams play, 27 Wagons of Cotton. Woman has her stomach tickled by the male star. Different tickling than seen in the play.

59. HOTS: A young woman is tied and gagged by a rival sorority and briefly tickled on ribs and knees.

60. CURTAINS: A woman trapped in an insane asylum is tickled on the torso by another female patient.

61. URBAN COWBOY: John Travolta tickles Debra Winger's ribs while playfully teasing her about being jealous.

62. ORANGES ARE NOT THE ONLY FRUIT: Two teenage girls have a tickle-wrestle in this adaptation of the wonderful novel about a young woman's coming of age.

63. THE ADVENTURES OF BARON MUNCHAUSEN: Robin Williams tickles the feet of his wife with a feather.

This is a somewhat strange scene; in the story his wife's head is actually with other people somewhere else (trust me, this is a film involving some of the Monty Python people).

64. LOVE AT FIRST BITE: Susan St. James' feet are licked by a dog. She giggles and playfully whines that it tickles. A somewhat similar, quick scene can be found in SHE-DEVIL and a slightly longer scene in ONCE UPON A HORSE. In THE PARENT TRAP, a woman's feet are tickled by a licking bear cub.

65. THE RAINBOW: A teenage woman giggles and accuses her female lover of tickling while being massaged in this adaptation of the D. H. Lawrence novel.

66. ABSOLUTE BEGINNERS: Two men are tied and briefly tickled with a feather duster by a woman.

67. THE WORLD ACCORDING TO GARP: Robin Williams tickles his wife's belly by drawing on her with a magic marker. There is a brief, similar scene in MILK MONEY.

68. THE TEACHER: A young man tickles the ribs of a woman who is attempting not to show a reaction. She finally gives in, reacts, and submits.

69. TWO FOR THE ROAD: Audrey Hepburn gets her ribs tickled in two cute scenes in this otherwise excellent movie.

70. THE CONCORDE: AIRPORT 1979: A young woman is briefly tickled by her boyfriend, who is hiding under

the water in her hot tub.

71. DON'T GO TO SLEEP: Valerie Harper gets her knees briefly tickled. She responds with laughter and begging.

72. GIRL ON A SWING: Meg Tilly shrieks as her stocking foot is briefly tickled during a doctor's examination. She apologizes for her ticklishness.

73. MAKING MR. RIGHT: John Malkovich tickles a woman's stockinged foot with his fingers and chin while giving a massage.

74. LOOK WHO'S TALKING TOO: Young boy takes the shoe off of, and tickles, an adult woman's stockinged foot while hiding under the table. The voice of Bruce Willis provides the verbal teasing.

75. LIES MY FATHER TOLD ME: Husband tickles his wife's ribs twice in one scene.

76. THE CEMENT GARDEN: Teenage boy tickles his sister in a longish (for the genre) scene that ends with her losing bladder control.

77. MONSTER ON THE CAMPUS: Quick scene in which a man tickles his girlfriends stomach.

78. VARIETY GIRL: A woman's feet are tickled to elicit real-sounding laughter for a soundtrack.

79. TAKEN AWAY: Valerie Bertinelli tickles her daughter.

67

80. Jessica Lange gets her ribs briefly tickled by Joan Cusak in Men Don't Leave.

Television tickles

There have been a variety of tickling scenes from television programs over the years, Lucy's accidental brief (and not shown) foot tickle by Ricky during "The handcuffs" episode of I Love Lucy, for example, or several classic scenes from The Avengers (check out episodes "The Fear Merchants" and "The Legacy of Death"). Most, however, are difficult to find since the shows are not rerun and the plots of the shows are no longer listed in the tv guides. We won't waste space by listing them, but will suggest hooking into one of the computer bulletin boards listed above to get tips for recent or upcoming television tickles that you will be likely to find.

Chapter 6: Tickling Fiction

We've included a few stories in this last section to give you some more ideas. Some of the stories are a little more fiction and a little less fact. Some are a little more fact and a little less fiction. We'll leave it to you to figure out which are which. We called the section fiction anyway since it's meant to be the jumping off point for fantasy and later play. We hope that the stories suggest some playful scenes for you to act out, and later to create your own.

An Evening at Home

Last night, I had the pleasure of having a fantasy within a fantasy come true. The larger fantasy, of being engaged in a truly loving relationship with a kind, caring, intelligent and very sexy man, is one that I have been fortunate enough to be living for some time now. Since he is characteristically concerned with my pleasure, the smaller fantasy was made reality too.

We had discussed the spy-interrogator scenario many times before. I have written other pieces similar to this one along those themes for him as well, and it became a popular fantasy of mine. I have discovered my submissive side through our relationship, and consider myself lucky to be training under such a loving and skilled master. The other thing I learned about myself

through our relationship is my love of being tickled by
my master. His feather-light fingertips or prodding
poking along my sides, down my legs, and on my feet not
only makes me laugh and squirm, but also become
incredibly turned on. The spy-interrogator scenario
exploits both of these erotic topics for me: as the
spy, I am helpless before the interrogator, brought to
submission by being tickled. That evening, as I drove
us to the gym, my master informed me that we would be
acting out my fantasy later that night.

The evening was pleasant. We got home from the
gym, both tired and a little sore. We had dinner in
front of the television, laughing together and bringing
each other pleasure. I massaged my master's calves,
enjoying the feel of his legs on my lap and his muscles
under my hands. When Star Trek ended, we took a shower
together. With the hot water beating upon my back and
my master's arms around me, I thought I must be in
heaven. He kissed my neck, sucking the water off my
skin and making me melt. I pressed against him,
returning the kisses. Eventually, we got down to the
business of actually washing, and took our leave of the
steamy bathroom.

I curled up upon the bed, observing my master. He
lit the two candles on the coffee table and a cone of
incense. Just as I was wondering when we would engage

in our scene, he came and laid down next to me. The candlelight flickered through the apartment as he said, "Now, isn't this intimate?"

I murmured my agreement, and he continued. "Now, why don't you tell me what you're doing in my apartment."

Now I understood. The game had begun. I shrugged casually, caught off-guard. "No."

"So you're burglarizing me and you won't tell me about it."

"I wasn't going to take anything," I protested.

"Were you going to leave something?"

"No. I was looking for something."

"Looking for what?"

"Doesn't matter. I think I'll be going now," I said, sitting up. I felt his hand firmly grasp my wrist. He roughly pulled me back onto the bed.

"But it does matter to me," he said. "I came home to find you in my apartment, looking for something, and I'd like to know what."

"Well, I can't tell you," I said. "So we really have nothing else to talk about. I'll be on my way."

I sat up again, and again he grabbed me and forced me back onto the bed. "Who sent you?"

"I don't know what you're talking about," I said coolly.

"Oh, so it's like that, huh?"

I didn't answer. "Is there anything else you'd like to know?"

"What's your favorite color?"

"Pink."

"Very feminine. I'll bet your bedroom is all pink, isn't it?"

"At one time it was," I replied. "Is that all now?"

He began to trace his finger along my side and down my leg. I tried to stay in character and shifted away from him. "Something wrong?" he asked.

"I really don't think it's your place to be doing that," I said, trying to be dignified.

"Well, whatever's in my apartment is mine. I found you here, so I guess you're mine and I can do whatever I want with you."

"I'm not yours," I said angrily, sitting up again. He pushed me back for a third time, holding my arm over my head. I began to get even more excited, feeling utterly helpless to him. Of course, I wasn't trying to leave for real, but I knew that his strength was such that if I really wanted to leave, and he wanted to stop me, there would be no contest.

"You're not leaving until you tell me what you were looking for," he said calmly. There was no menace

72

in his voice. There never was. My submission was never brought about by fear, but by trust.

"Since you've been searching through my apartment, I assume you've seen the restraints tied around the legs of my bed." I nodded. "What do you think they're there for?"

"Dominance and submission games," I said.

He nodded. "That's correct. You said you're not mine. Are you a sub?"

"Yes," I replied. "But not to you."

"You might beg to be," he said, continuing to stroke me. I shivered. "I'll bet your master is just a wannabe. Dominance and submission relationships are built upon trust. Are you familiar with the concept of safewords?"

"Yes," I said. "But I can't trust you. You're angry with me."

"I'm not angry," he said. "And I won't hurt you. That's not the way civilized people conduct themselves. I just want to know what you were looking for."

"Well, I'm not telling you," I said stubbornly. "You can do whatever you want, but I'm not telling."

"Did you ever read George Orwell's _1984_?"

"Room 101."

"That's right. I'm going to find out what's in your Room 101," he said. I shivered with delight. In

73

fact, we both knew what was in Room 101, or at least one of the things, but his efforts to "discover" it would be quite pleasurable.

"I haven't found my own Room 101 yet," I laughed. "I don't think you will. I can take whatever you have to give."

"Really," he said. "What if I got one of those candles from over there and singed your flesh?"

I shrugged.

"What if I raped you?"

Again, a casual shake of my head.

"You've been raped?"

I squirmed, shifting the hip that his fingertip was slowly tracing along.

"I'll make you talk," he warned.

"I've been very well trained," I said, stretching.

"Well, I don't really trust anyone else. We'll see how well you've been trained."

Now his lazy stroking turned into little flicking motions. His fingers danced along my ribs and down my sides. I stiffened, trying my best to hide my reaction. Laughter caught in my throat and I struggled against the urge to squirm.

I guess I wasn't doing such a good job of hiding my ticklishness, because he said, "What's the problem?"

"No problem," I gasped, as his fingers continued

74

to torture my sides and belly.

"Are you ticklish?"

"Just a little," I said. "It won't work, so don't bother."

"Are you sure about that?"

"Yes," I squealed, as he tickled under my arms and along the sides of my breasts. I couldn't help it anymore, and I erupted into full-blown laughter, complete with jumping and squirming. The more he tickled me, the more aroused I became. I could feel the fire between my legs building as my flesh became ever more sensitive.

When we first began our relationship, I was extremely ticklish. My reactions were heightened; I couldn't handle being tickled for too long. As time went on, however, and my master never failed to stop his tickling before it became true torture, I grew to trust him more and more. Now my trust in him and in his concern for my pleasure is so absolute that ticklishness has decreased in intensity. I can bear and in fact invite greater lengths of time at his fingertips. Sometimes I miss the old sensitivity, but I am glad for the new way I react to tickle. It permits more tickling and most importantly, it is a symbol of the depth that our relationship has reached.

Tonight, however, my sensitivity was much stronger

than usual. I was laughing louder and squirming more. Perhaps it was the role I was playing. I was very much into my character, who hadn't established any trust with his character. I welcomed the temporary renewal of my hyper-sensitivity.

"Want to talk?" he cooed.

"Nope," I giggled, struggling against him.

"This would be much easier if you were restrained," he said. "Would you mind?"

"Do I have a choice?"

"Not really. You aren't going to fight me, are you? I don't want to struggle with you."

"I don't think it would do any good," I pointed out. "You're much bigger than me and stronger than me. If you want me tied up, there's not much I can do about it."

This, too, was a turn-on. I couldn't stop him even if I wanted to. Without even being tied up, I was helpless. I became even more aroused as he slipped the velcro bands around my ankles and wrists.

"There's another way to heighten your sensitivity," he mused, plucking the blindfold from the end table behind my head. "Okay?"

I remained cool. As a slave, I was eager for the blindfold. The deprivation of my sight would increase my ticklishness and the tension of the moment that so excited me. I wouldn't know where the next touch would come from, or what it would consist of. As a spy, I would show no fear or resistance. If he knew he was getting to me in any way, he would persist until I gave in.

The blindfold was secured over my eyes. My interrogator inquired after my comfort, and with a few adjustments to take the pressure of the elastic band off of my ear, I indicated that I was quite comfortable.

The tickling began again. "Is there anywhere else that you're ticklish?" he teased.

"No," I lied.

"Are you sure? Aren't your feet ticklish?"

"No," I said firmly.

"I don't know. It seems that the lower I go, the more ticklish you get," he said, moving his wiggling fingers down my side and the top of my thigh.

I laughed, squirming in protest. I tried my hardest to conceal my more intense reaction to his fingers on my legs, even though I knew that in reality he knew all of my most ticklish spots. In fact, I even knew that he was saving the worst for last, and that he was prolonging the game. My master knew where to touch me to get me completely within his control.

"Maybe I should try tickling your feet," he

suggested.

"No!" I protested.

"Why not?"

"I lied," I said desperately. "My feet are very ticklish. Please don't tickle me there."

"All you have to do is tell me what you were looking for," he said softly.

"No," I said firmly. "Do whatever you want. I won't tell."

"Have it your way," he sighed, and lay across my legs, facing my vulnerable feet.

His fingertips on my soles and between my toes had me shrieking with laughter. "Wanna talk?" he'd coo occasionally.

I'd toss back some comment like, "About what? The weather?"

"So you're a smartass, huh?" he'd say, tickling me even more.

I was loving this. The more he tickled me, the more excited I became. I knew that he was enjoying it, too, since he kept doing it. He knew just how to end the game, but was taking his time getting there. Knowing that my master was deriving pleasure from this game as well got me even more turned on.

Eventually, he stopped tickling me feet and got off my legs. I caught my breath, feeling the sweat of my exertions drying and my muscles relaxing. I felt his hand between my legs, stroking me, and I moaned out loud.

"Is this getting you hot?" he asked.

"Oh, yes," I moaned.

He withdrew his hand. "Do you want more?"

"Yes, please," I whimpered.

"Just tell me what I want to hear."

"No," I sighed.

He tortured me next with a feather, running it along my soles and between my toes. Up and down my legs, making me laugh and twitch on the bed, tugging at my restraints. When he stroked my belly and breasts with it, I arched upward towards the softness. "Feels good," I whispered. More tickling, and I refused to give up each time he asked me if I felt like talking.

Finally I felt what I knew would be the end of my willpower: his hand upon my neck. I lost my breath, my body stiffened, my head craned towards my shoulders. With the lightest touch, I lost all control. "Please, please, please, no, don't," I begged, hardly able to get the words out. It was so ticklish I couldn't even laugh.

"Don't give me please," he said. "Do you want to talk?"

I hesitated for an instant. "Move your hands, and

we'll talk."

"Not good enough."

"Okay, okay!" I gasped. "I'll talk. I'll tell you. Just move your hands, please!"

"Now I don't know if I want to hear," he said. "I'm enjoying this."

"Oh, please, please!" I begged.

"Beg me to let you talk," he suggested.

"Please let me tell you my secret," I pleaded.

"Please who?"

"Please . . . master."

"Okay." He moved his hand from my neck, resting his arm across my chest. His hand remained too close to my sensitive neck, causing my skin to tingle in a most distracting way.

"Please move your hand," I said.

"No, I think I'll keep it here for insurance," he replied.

"Oh, please," I said. "You can move it back up quickly enough if I don't talk."

"You have a point," he said, and moved his hand. "Now talk. You aren't going to lie to me, are you?"

"No, I won't lie," I said. "I was hired by your employer to look for information about other businesses that you were interested in."

"That's plausible," he said. "Why not just ask me

in the first place?"

"I don't know. They hired me to do a job, and that's all I know."

"Why wouldn't you just tell me this?"

"Because I'm paid to do these things secretly. I owe it to my client."

"Well, your client really wouldn't care if he knew that you were in this position right now," he said kindly.

My master slipped his hands between my legs, where I was slippery wet. "Now you can stay or you can go," he said.

"I'll stay," I breathed, flooded with pleasure as he stroked me.

"Do you give yourself freely?" he asked.

"Yes."

"Who is your master now?"

"You are."

"And your old master?"

"Forgotten."

"Will this fate ever befall me?"

"Never, master."

"For how long will you serve me?"

"For as long as you'll have me, master."

As I reaffirmed my slave status through these questions and answers, the sweet desire grew ever stronger. My position as his slave is very important and exciting to me, and these reminders make me feel not only aroused, but also loved and safe. He continued to stroke me, stoking the fires. I lost myself to this long-awaited pleasure, feeling my legs grow tense as my orgasm approached. Soon, I was climaxing with a vengeance. I ground against his hand, my vaginal muscles contracting around the finger that he had slipped inside of me when my orgasm began. As usual, the orgasm left me bereft of energy but wholly fulfilled, feeling as though I was floating in some magical place.

My master removed my blindfold and untied me. I slowly drew my arms down and my legs together, feeling the sweet stiffness in my muscles. I felt his warm arms around me, embraced him back. This was pure happiness; this was peace. I fell asleep, knowing that I was the luckiest woman in the world.

We awoke early the next morning; he had to work, I had a class. On these early mornings, there wasn't time for the usual wake-up playtime, so we dressed quickly and separately, stumbling around, half-awake and getting ready to go. Before we left, though, he sat next to me on the bed and kissed me. I felt him pushing me down onto my back, closed my eyes and lost myself in his kiss and his embrace. I felt him hard against me, rubbed up to meet him. Instantly, I was hot, and became hotter still when he tickled my ribs a little.

"Are you turned on now?" he murmured in my ear.

"Yes, master," I sighed.

"Poor baby," he sang, tickling me some more. "You may make yourself come when you get home. You have an assignment, though. I want a written account of your experience, beginning with when we got home last night and ending now. Do you understand?"

"Yes, master," I replied. "I understand."

The Wrestlers

We love to watch wrestling together on television. Not the fake, professional kind, but the real wrestling you see in the Olympics. I had competed in high school and in college and she had fallen in love with the sport even as we fell in love with each other. Sometimes when we watch we get playful with each other and start to wrestle. I'm a great deal larger and stronger than her, so I shouldn't have any problem with her. But I do. You see, she knows a weakness of mine and has a hold I don't know a counter for. It's a tickle hold.

Yes, I'm terribly ticklish. It's a weakness that was exploited at every opportunity by my sister when I was growing up, and it was she who told my lover how to keep me in line. I've tried all the tricks people talk about to stop being ticklish, but to this day there's almost no spot on my body that isn't ticklish. My sides, stomach and legs are bad, but my feet and under my arms are absolute torture. Of course, those are the spots she goes for.

She keeps me in pretty good check that way. If I disagree with her, especially in public, and she's in the mood to assert her dominance, all she needs to do is covertly bicycle her fingers near me and I knuckle under. She has threatened to tell her friends, and mine, how ticklish I am so that they will all have this power over me. I beg her not to, and usually we can negotiate some service on my part to buy her silence.

Before you ask, she's also ticklish. The problem is that she can control herself. Truth is, I think she likes it. I can't win a tickle fight, and trying to assert myself in this way just gets me tickled worse. I thought about tying her up once, but I know she'd get me back all the worse once she was free. I'm afraid I'm helpless. Don't get me wrong, I love this woman and she loves me. She just enjoys making me giggle and squirm, to be "her helpless little boy." What the hell, it turns her on and sometimes I can get into it too.

Then there are the other times. Once, to buy her

silence regarding my vulnerability during a visit by some of her girlfriends (picturing four sets of long nails torturing me was just too much), I had to agree to be her slave for an evening. I got into my role and enjoyed serving her in all sorts of ways that evening. Hell, she deserves some pampering sometimes. She does enough for me. Then came the dreaded order to strip and to lay down on the bed so that I could be bound.

Once tied, I tried to strike up conversation to distract her from paying attention to my vulnerable spots. It didn't work. After about two minutes, she began to wiggle her fingers a couple of inches over my hypersensitive belly. That's when I knew I was done for. "What's wrong, sweetie?" she cooed. "You seem to be so nervous, can't breathe straight. Are you ok?"

I didn't answer, trying to steel myself. With a sadistic grin on her face she slowly lowered her fingertips onto heaving belly. Her grin got even wider as she teased, "Tickle, tickle, tickle! I've got you now! C'mon, giggle for me, little boy!"

I, of course, burst into hysterical giggles and begged for mercy. To my great surprise, in a short time I got some. She pulled back and I managed to regain my breath. "That wasn't so bad, was it?" I didn't dare answer. If I said no, she might say, "Oh, so I need to do it harder!" If I said yes, she might be angry for not being properly appreciative that she hadn't done worse. She figured out a way around my silence. She walked down to my feet.

"Cat got your tongue? Well, you're going to talk. Recite this little piggy for me!" she demanded deviously. What a terrible bit of psychology! I would be forced to tease myself, knowing that when the tease was done my feet would be tortured. "Recite or it'll be A LOT worse on you" she warned. Of course I complied.

One by one my toes were playfully kneaded. What I most dreaded finally happened. She reached the last toe, and then the tickling began. As I burst into tortured giggles, the inevitable happened. I felt an erection forming. This, of course, was not lost on her. "You love this, don't you? Tell me you love it. Tell me!"

Of course, I had no choice but to admit it. With my erection so full that it hurt, she suddenly changed tactics. She left my feet alone, got on top of me, and took me inside her. The rush of pleasure was suddenly overwhelming as she dug her fingertips into my ribs and underarms. "Just to keep you moving," she teased into my ear. My torment/pleasure lasted for only a couple of minutes. Her orgasm touched off my own. As always, I came so hard that the muscles in my legs and arms nearly pulled.

The tickling became more sensuous as my haze cleared. The probing turned into feathery caresses. Our eyes met, and she looked love, contentment, and a lifetime of togetherness into my eyes. "I love you, little boy." She beamed her mischievous smile at me, showing me that I was no little boy and she knew it. Meaning every word of it, I replied, "I love you, too."

The Interrogation

I climbed into my car on a hot, sticky Thursday, and it was hotter than any oven has ever been. I immediately rolled down both windows and drove off as fast as I could, trying to circulate the sea breezes through my car. I was finished work for the day, had the next two days off, and was on my way to a rendezvous. Life was good, even if the heat was oppressive.

I was at my destination a convenient five minutes later, not sorry to leave my car to bake further in the sun. I expected not to enter it again until the following morning, by which time it should have cooled off. In the meantime, I looked forward to a relaxing evening of good company, backrubs, foot massages, and possibly some unpredictably exciting stimulation.

I let myself into an empty apartment and collapsed onto the bed after slipping out of my sweaty shorts and shoes. A cool breeze through the terrace door was circulated by the fan, and I dozed off in a few minutes, exhausted from the day's work.

It was only a few minutes later that I heard the door open and close. The sound penetrated the light sleep I had fallen into, and I rolled over lazily, expecting a kiss and a hug, and a decent interval of salutary cuddling. Instead, I was greeted by a strange woman.

"Oh," I said, startled, sitting up. I was suddenly aware that I was only wearing my tank top and panties, and I self-consciously reached for my shorts.

"Sorry to startle you," she said. "Don't bother, really."

I was halted by this strange command. "Who are you?" I asked stupidly, not sure if I should be scared.

"I'm a friend of Pete'. I presume you're Jan?"

"Uh, yes," I said. "I'm sorry, I didn't catch your name."

She smiled and shook her head. "I didn't offer it." She seated herself on the couch, turned in my direction. I remained frozen on the bed.

"I'd like to talk to you," she said.

Now I was beginning to worry. Was this a psycho ex-girlfriend who still had his keys? No matter, he would be home any minute now. In the meantime, I would

just talk to her. He'd be here to settle this in no
time at all.

"Actually, I just want to ask you something," she
continued, ignoring my silence. "Well, to be more
accurate, Pete wants me to ask you something."

Now I knew she was nuts. If Pete wanted to know
something, he would ask me himself. "What is it?" I
asked, trying to smile.

"How long have you and he been seeing each other?"
she asked.

I laughed nervously. "Is that the question?"

"Yes, it is."

"Well, he certainly knows the answer," I replied.
"Why would he send you to ask me such a thing?"

She smiled. "Just answer the question."

"No, that's ridiculous," I said. "He can ask me
anything and be assured of my honesty, and besides,
that's a worthless question. Maybe you'd better go
now."

"Answer the question," she said firmly.

Now I was in a quandary. I didn't have the
faintest idea who this woman was, and I wasn't about to
give away any incriminating information to a perfect
stranger. I was sure that he wouldn't send someone to
burst in on me and ask me such a strange thing, but she
was obviously unstable and had to be handled

delicately. I decided to bluff.

"A month," I said.

"Now how about the truth?" she asked gently.

My head spun. Had she been spying on us? Anything was possible at this point. Would lying further compound the problem? I had no choice.

"Really," I said. "Just about a month." I reached for my shorts again, but she was up off the couch in a flash. She snatched the shorts from my hands.

"I said, don't bother," she repeated. "He told me you might be difficult about this."

"I'm sure he did," I said, wondering where the hell he was. He should have been here ten minutes ago, at least, I thought frantically.

"Now, will you talk to me nicely?" she asked. "We have ways of making you talk, my dear," she laughed. "I know a lot about you."

"Uh-huh," I said, trying to stall for time. "By the way, you still didn't tell me your name. How can I talk to you without knowing your name?"

She shrugged. "There's no need to address me. It's just you and me here."

I got up off the bed.

"Sit," she said sharply.

"I was just going to get some soda," I said,

sitting back down.

"I'm not thirsty," she said.

"I am," I replied.

"Answer my question and I'll be on my way and you can have all the soda you want," she said reasonably.

"I answered you," I protested.

"Not truthfully."

"Well, if you know the truth, why are you asking me?" I reasoned.

"I'm the one asking the questions here, not you," she said.

My blood boiled. Who was this strange woman interfering in my life and giving me an attitude to boot? And where was Pete when I needed him?

"Last chance, sweetie," she said. "You want give me an honest answer or not?"

Last chance? She was going then. "I've given you an honest answer," I said, relaxing as she stood up. Hasta la vista.

But no, she was heading towards me.

She was easily five inches taller and thirty pounds heavier than me. When she threw me onto my back and sat on my legs, there wasn't much my struggling could do. "Have it your way," she sighed.

"Let me go," I said furiously, sitting up and pushing at her. I bucked my legs, but to no avail.

She put one hand on my chest and pushed me down.

"He said I wasn't to hurt you," she said. "But he's not here, is he?"

She leaned over the side of the bed and retrieved one of the velcro restraints that were tied around each leg of the bed. She knew they were there, supporting a crazy ex-girlfriend theory. Oh, God, let him get home soon, I prayed, as I struggled against her hand firmly clamped around my ankle and felt the nylon loop being slipped over my foot. This was usually an exciting feeling, but then again, it wasn't usually being done by a strange, psychotic woman.

Despite my struggles and my pleas, she had me completely bound in a short period of time. "Let me go!" I yelled. "Damn you! Who do you think you are? Just wait until he gets home! He'll be here any minute!"

She laughed. "You think so. He'll be here about ten minutes after I'm done with you, and I won't be done until I get the truth from you. Have you changed your mind?"

I narrowed my eyes at her. I ignore her. How much worse could she get?

"What a dirty look," she mused. "Those eyes are on fire. Better protect myself." She reached over my head for the blindfold that had been carelessly left on the end table at the head of the bed. Well, who really expected a crazy woman to break in and use it on me?

"No, please, no," I begged, stepping on my own plan. She slipped it over my head anyway, and I was plunged into total darkness.

"Please let me go," I whimpered, thrashing around uselessly. I knew that my efforts were futile, being familiar with these bonds under happier circumstances, but I tried anyway.

"What's it worth to you?"

The words sent a chill up my spine. He always said that to me. "Not what you want," I said firmly. I could bear this out. He would be home at any moment. I wouldn't back down now.

"Okay," she said simply, and I felt her weight leave the bed. She was soundless in her movements, if she moved at all. I couldn't fathom where she might be, if she was still beside me, or if she was wandering around the apartment. My head spun with fear. I was helpless before this sadistic stranger. I couldn't even see my protagonist. I had no idea what she was going to do. I held on to my certainty that he would show up at any moment and get me out of this, and tried to slow my breathing to a more normal pace.

Suddenly, I felt the scrape of one fingernail being trailed slowly up the sole of my foot, from heel to toes. My back arched and a scream erupted from my throat. As the scream died away, I heard her chuckle.

"He said your feet are very ticklish."

"Bull!" I cried. "It was a lucky guess. Why would he send you to ask me something that he already knows? He wouldn't do this to me!"

"He also said you were bright," she replied. "I would think you would figure this out by now."

"Well, I think it's just that you're crazy!" I exploded. Suddenly a new and immensely fearsome thought crossed my mind. What if she had somehow detained him? What if she had him tied up somewhere? What if he wasn't coming after all?

The fingernail visited my sole again. "No," I moaned, laughing and bucking on the bed. My foot spasmed in its collar, and my head thrashed from side to side. There was nothing sensual about this tickle. There was nothing playful about it, and it was far from the usual turn-on. Of course, tickle is only a turn-on for me when delivered by the right person in the right way. And where was that person, anyway?

"Maybe," she suggested in a voice of pure honey, "I have been employed by your master to test your devotion and your endurance."

"Impossible," I burst out, struggling to get away from her teasing fingernails. But a seed was planted in my mind.

As she continued to torture my feet, I tossed the idea around. No, it was crazy. He wouldn't do this to me. Simply impossible. Further clear thought was impossible; my mind was hazy with fear and with the tickling, which was becoming almost painful in its persistence.

"He said I should give you a break," she said, ceasing her wiggling fingers. "I suppose I should let you catch your breath."

Relieved, I relaxed against the bed. Maybe this insanity was coming to an end. A moment later, there was the unmistakable sound of the door opening and closing. I tensed again, hopeful. He was finally home. "Pete?"

No answer. "Hello? Someone? Anyone?"

Panic rose in me, a physical sensation in my throat and chest. "Hello? Help!" I screamed, struggling again. I was alone. This was truly a nightmare. I half wished she was back. No one was expecting me home for several hours, really not until the next day. I could be left here for an interminable amount of time, bound and blindfolded. What if there was a fire? I suddenly felt very thirsty, and thought of a terrible Steven King novel I had read not long ago about a woman who was trapped in handcuffs on her bed for days.

Suddenly, I heard laughter. "Thought I left you, huh?" she asked, beside me again.

"You bitch!" I screamed, furious that she had done this to me, and seen me in my futile struggles, screaming in panic.

"Wouldn't you like to get up?"

"Let me go!" I ordered, trying to sit up and getting caught up short by the bonds.

"Talk to me," she said.

"No!"

"Fine. Cootchie-cootchie-coo!" she trilled, and I felt the hateful fingers flickering up my sides, under my tank top which she pushed up on her way up my ribs.

"No, stop!" I begged, laughing helplessly and jerking uncontrollably.

"Ah, I know," she said. "He said this would do it."

As she rested her fingertips ever so lightly on the back of my neck, my breath stopped. "No, no, no!" I moaned.

The fingertips moved slightly. "No!" I gasped, my whole body rigid. "Please, please!"

She began to tickle the back of my neck, and I screamed in agony. I realized that he had to be in on this. She knew me too well. In a matter of seconds, my brain put together the realization that she knew all of my most ticklish spots and my fear of being bound and blindfolded and left alone, and that she had used several familiar phrases. This was indeed a test.

"I'll tell!" I cried.

Her fingers stopped moving. "Tell."

"Move your hands," I gasped, barely able to summon my breath enough to get the sentence out.

She moved her hands, and I talked. "Since about the middle of July," I admitted.

"Good. Thanks," she said. "That's all you needed to say. Although I must say, it's been fun finding out. You put up a good struggle."

I felt her remove the velcro strap from my left wrist. "You can handle the rest yourself," she said.

I lay there stunned for a moment, hearing the door open and close again. I ripped off the blindfold and assured myself through blurry eyes that she was gone.

She was. Ten minutes, she said. Ten minutes after she finished, he would arrive. I was both furious and suddenly turned on. I wondered if I should bother untying myself.

The Spy

I've been caught. My cover's blown - they know just what I've been up to. They know that I have the information they need. At least they don't know my real name. That much is mine.

And now here I am, sitting defensively, posture straight and proud, chin jutting defiantly, while he circles my chair. He is smiling, confident that he will learn my secret. After all, he is a specialist, just like me. Spy versus interrogator.

I stare straight ahead, refusing to admit my anxiety by looking at his face or at my surroundings. You've brought me here, I think, but you can't make me be here. On one of his trips past me, however, I catch a silver flash in his hand. A knife. Dear God.

He stops, finally, in front of my chair. I stare straight ahead, silent and stoic. I am gazing sightlessly at the front of his shirt until he brings the knife into my line of vision. I continue to stare unflinchingly, dispassionately noting the way the light gleams off of the razor-sharp blade.

He lifts the knife and with every bit of self-control that I can muster, I remain perfectly still as he slowly and lightly traces the point from my temple to my chin. For the first time, he speaks. "Your skin would melt like butter under this knife," he murmurs, almost adoringly.

My breath catches as he draws the blade down my throat, resting it in the tender hollow of my collarbone. Between my breasts, slowly, finally resting the point directly into my quivering stomach. "One quick push," he says. "Would you like to tell me anything?" He jabs the knife so that I can feel its bite, but it doesn't puncture my skin.

I call his bluff. "No." I know that what he wants from me can't be taken if I'm dead.

He doesn't withdraw the threat immediately, however. He lets the blade drop so that it is pressed between my legs and then slowly drags it down the inside of my thigh.

"I know what you're thinking," he says. "You think I won't kill you because then you can't talk. Know what? You're right. Killing is so mindless anyway, simply no fun. Besides, there's no need for that. Did you ever read 1984?"

My mind races. I know what he means.

"Room 101," I think and he says aloud. "The place with the worst thing in the world. You see, everybody has a weakness. One thing they can't stand. Death, pain, that they can stand. But there's that one intolerable thing." He pauses for emphasis. "My job is to find that one thing, and I'm better at it than anyone. I know this isn't what my dissertation committee had in mind for me when I completed my doctorate, but one never knows where life will lead, does one?"

He resumes his work. With one hand, he removes my shoe and gently places the blade between my first and second toes. My foot twitches as I imagine the sharp knife slicing the delicate web of skin. My foot also twitches for physical reasons. My feet have always been sensitive.

"She doesn't scare so easily," he says to himself. "Oh, this can be a lot of fun. Did I just see what I thought I saw? No harm in finding out. This is a science after all."

He stands and slips the knife into its sheath at his side. I feel his hand encircling my arm, lifting me from my chair.

"You have beautiful skin," he says. "I'd like to see more of it."

I close my eyes as he unbuttons my blouse and it drops to the floor. He unhooks my bra, tugs down my jeans and panties. When I am naked, I open my eyes to find him surveying my body. I won't cringe. I won't speak. He puts his hand on my breast and I set my jaw more firmly.

"What if I raped you?" he says. "Wouldn't you rather just tell me a few sweet secrets than have them raped out of you?"

One clipped word. "No." And I silently say to myself "You bastard."

He laughs at me. "That's okay. By the time we're done, you'll be begging for it."

He takes my wrist and starts to pull, but I walk willingly. I won't let him know how terrified I am, how vulnerable I feel. I won't let him know that he's affecting me at all.

I am being pushed onto a bed. So he's going to rape me after all. How amateurish, I had expected better of him. One of the perks of being a female spy. It's happened before. This actually gives me confidence. Maybe he isn't as creative as I had feared.

But no, he's going to do this right. He takes my feet and shoves them into restraints tied at the corners of the bed. When he ties up my hands, one by one, I can't help but to pull back a little.

"Careful, you're cracking," he teases.

I am spread on this bed, naked and at the mercy of this stranger who is my adversary. There is no way out. Well, one way. I could talk.

I bite my tongue to keep the secret in as he slips a blindfold over my eyes. Oh, God, now I can't even see what's coming. I can't know what torture he will choose to inflict on me, I can't run, I can't fight. I can only speak.

There is nothing for a long time. I wait

interminable minutes, straining to hear some movement or indication of where he is. For all I know, he is standing over me, watching as I hold my muscles tense in an effort to keep from struggling against the restraints.

A noise. A sound. It is a buzzing, harsh, grating sound. It is getting closer and louder. A thousand images pass through my mind. An electric drill or knife. A circular saw or sander. "What is it?" I hiss through dry lips.

"A secret for a secret," he offers, and there is a thud on the mattress between my legs, the buzzing is right there. I don't know the parameters of it. One move and something could happen - I don't even know what.

"I won't tell," I say through gritted teeth. You won't beat me at this, I say to myself furiously. I'll call your bluff again.

"It was worth a try," he says, and the buzzing is gone. "Excuse me."

The weight is gone from the mattress and I hear his footsteps receding. I am thrown once more into a whirlwind of waiting, anxiety building with every blessed minute that he is gone. I debate with myself: is it better to remain like this, under this incredible tension, or to endure whatever is next? I cannot come to an answer, and it's not like I have a choice, anyway.

I hear footsteps approaching, and with straining ears, I discern two pairs of feet. Oh, what would it take two people to do to one totally helpless, bound person?

I hear him talking to this new stranger. I don't even know what he looks like. At least I can picture the first one in my mind.

"I thought you would get a kick out of this," I hear him saying to his companion. "You do it so well."

I am shocked at the sound of the new voice. A woman? For some reason, there is a slightly greater degree of shame and anxiety in knowing that a woman is seeing me like this.

"Are you sure that she'll respond?" she's asking.

"I have a feeling," he says. "Watch this." Suddenly, on my little toe, there is the sensation of pressure, and ridges. He has a pair of pliers and is squeezing with the slightest amount of pressure. Not enough to hurt, but enough to let me know it could. I twitch again. My feet are so sensitive.

"Try it." Try what? I brace for the pressure to build up blindingly painful proportions.

Try what? I want to scream.

They fall silent and I wait, suddenly wishing that

I was waiting for their approach again. This is infinitely more torturous.

My whole body bucks on the mattress as the lightest scrape of fingernails is applied to the sole of my foot.

They laugh. "How about that, a ticklish spy," the woman says mockingly.

His coarser fingers are on my ribs, digging and walking up my sides, making me writhe and gasp. She runs her nails up my calves, stopping to tease the backs of my knees, making me instinctively try to draw my knees up. Of course, I am stopped short by the tug of the restraints at my ankles. I try to imagine those nails, and see crimson daggers jutting from the ends of slender white fingers.

Every inch of my skin is hypersensitive with the fear and anxiety; the merest touch sends a vibration through my body. I hold myself as still as possible, hoping to convince them that I am not nearly as ticklish as I know I am, but whimpers tear from my throat.

They are finding all of the spots. Her feather touch on my hips, sending my back into an involuntary arch. His rougher grasp of my knee, causing my whole leg to convulse. They are laughing at me, teasing me.

"This little piggy went to market."

"And this little piggy stayed home."

The feeling of her nails on my toes is enough to make me laugh, but knowing what will happen when she gets to the last little piggy is making me squirm spasmodically.

"This little piggy had roast beef."

"And this little piggy had none."

There is a pause. It seems like forever. Then, suddenly, I feel my little toe being kneaded, and a cooing voice asking,

"Do you know what this last little piggy did?"

I try to remain silent, biting my lip. Isolated giggles escape, humiliating me, and betraying my weakness. "He went....WEE WEE WEE ALL THE WAY HOME!" Ten long nails dance on my soles, sending me into convulsions of laughter and spasms of movement.

"Can't get away, can you?" says the woman in her musical voice. "Koochie koo!" She teases me like a child, trying to highlight my helplessness. It works.

"We can do this for hours," the man reminds me. "It doesn't take much effort."

"All tied up and no place to go," the woman says in a mockingly sad voice. "Just think, we get paid by the hour."

They explode into laughter, and I am fuming. That such a gentle, silly touch could do this to me is humiliating. My gasps and chokes of laughter that have nothing to do with humor joins their chuckling, and we are all laughing together, spy and interrogator and interrogator.

"Give up?" the man says, probing my sensitive underarms.

"No," I moan through hysterics, denying the feeling. I try to push away this buzzing, this humming half-pleasure, half-pain, certainly unbearable feeling at their touch.

"Please stop," I cry out, as she returns to my feet, running her fingernails languorously from heel to toes and back down, along the sensitive sides and to the vulnerable little patch of skin near my ankle. "Please don't do this," I beg, hating the tears in my voice, as I continue to jump and squirm and he plays his fingertips across my stomach and under my arms.

"Just tell us your secret," the woman says soothingly, not ceasing her ministrations to my feet.

"No," I gasp.

"Have it your way," she says, poking my twitching, tortured feet.

All at once, they stop, and I remain tense for a few minutes. Slowly, my muscles relax, and my breathing returns to normal. Just as I am beginning to calm down, a scream erupts from my throat as twenty fingers again violate my skin, and they are all over me, inside of my thighs, along my upper back and the back of my neck, at my toes and behind my knees, on each rib and along the undersides of my arms. They tease me like a child again. Through my fog I hear koochies and piggies and cooing noises.

"Do you see what I see?" I hear the woman saying, and I know she's not talking to me. I can't see a thing.

"I think our spy has given us another clue," the man says. I feel his hand pressing between my legs, and he smears the wetness that he has collected across my face.

"Do we turn you on?" the woman says.

I won't answer. I won't admit to this final humiliation; this weakness. What kind of a spy gets turned on during an interrogation? How weak am I?

Their touch changes suddenly. No longer jerking away, I find myself pressing upward, against his hands lightly and slowly being drawn up the sides of my breasts. Her tickle has changed to a sensuous massage of my feet. I moan as her darting tongue flickers across my toes. My feet have betrayed me again.

Their hands travel over my body again, this time with open palms and a warm, melting touch. I try to steel myself against the insane pleasure. I try to remind myself to be afraid, but it feels too good. Defection suddenly seems like a viable option.

Her soft hands travel up the insides of my thighs. I feel the bite of her fingernails on the tender cushion at the base of my bottom. "Bad spy, making our bed all wet," she says in a low drawl.

"Who do you want?" the man asks. "Do you want a man, or do you want to find out what a woman can do to you?"

I bite my lip. I don't have to speak to them.

"I bet you've never had a woman," she says. "Poor thing. Are you scared?"

Yes, I answer silently.

"Just talk to us a little and you can have both," she offers.

"Both at once, or one at a time, in any order you choose," he says.

I could endure their touch all night. They handle me so expertly, each in their different ways, that I think I could come for hours.

I feel his rough fingertips on one of my aching nipples, and just as a low moan escapes me, her softer, nail-tipped fingers are on my other nipple.

"Please," I whisper, for the second time begging.

"We like to hear you talk," he says, and they continue their stroking for endless minutes. My arms, legs, hips, stomach, breasts. He slides his hands under my butt and squeezes as she runs her fingernails up my thighs.

Suddenly, they are there, between my legs. I cry out in ecstacy as he jams a finger into me while she gently strokes my clitoris. I can feel my own wetness running down my thighs. I can feel an orgasm approaching; just as I am at the brink, they stop.

"No! Don't stop!" I demand.

Their wonderful hands are gone.

"Talk," she says.

"No," I whimper, my resolve less certain.

"Just tell us this one thing," she says softly, resuming her stroking of my thighs.

"We can make you feel better than you've ever felt," he promises, cupping one of my breasts in each of his hands.

This time, as he stimulates my nipples, she is between my legs with her tongue. She passes over the sensitive peak of my clitoris several times, exploring me thoroughly with her warm, wet mouth. As I again teeter on the brink of coming, they abruptly stop.

A sob catches in my throat. "Oh, please, please," I moan, unable to even come up with a coherent request.

"We want to make you come," he says. "I'll bet it's beautiful."

"But we can't," she says. "Not until you talk."

I try my hardest to escape this situation, in my mind at least. I think of my duty to keep the secret. I think of the repercussions for giving it up. I set my jaw again and vow not to talk.

Fingers again, countless fingers stroking me. Fingers pulling the wetness from deep inside and painting my thighs and breasts with it, spreading it across my lips. I've never tasted myself before. It is infinitely exciting.

I am swept away in a whirlwind of excitement, unable to tell his fingers from hers, tongue from fingertip, where I begin and they end. Just as I am about to come, they stop again, but I find myself talking, spilling the secret, I just don't care anymore. I don't care what I am saying as the wonderful touch comes back and I explode, continuing to talk. I keep telling them more and more as I come again and again, words interspersed with moans as I writhe with indescribable pleasure. It is as though I am coming apart, and I don't care what happens, just as long as this white, melting heat continues to course through my body.

The orgasms seem to last for hours, my flesh tingling all over as my body shudders with spasms. When it finally ends, I gasp with the even more increased sensitivity of my skin, relieved when they take their hands away. I lay there, for a moment forgetting what I have done, feeling like I am floating as the clapping convulsions of the muscles in my vagina slowly fade away.

The blindfold is pulled off, and I face my interrogators, staring at them through blurry eyes. They are smiling at me.

"Thank you," she says. "You obviously can't go home now. Would you care to join our interrogator's training school, and make this a trio?" and licks her lips. I lick mine at the thought. "The pay's not great, but the benefits are unbelievable."
Orwell had a lot to learn.

The Gathering

We love to get together with Monica. She's an intelligent person of deep convictions and ethics. On top of that, she's a lot of fun to be with. Individually, we were all friends and had been since before Jan and I were a couple. When we became a couple, Monica remained as great a friend to the couple as she had been to the individuals. Pretty rare.

We had always been pretty physical with each other, and, thankfully, that continued. Our individual massages that we always gave to one another turned to group massages. There's little in the world that can compare to the feeling of two pairs of loving hands massaging you, or helping to massage another, with a deep feelings of affection for both of the people you're with. Maybe you love one romantically and the other one as a friend, but the depth of emotion and the feelings of warmth, trust, and comfort is something everyone should experience. We're all there, in times of crisis, in times of joy, in times of plenty and in the leaner times. We've even shared living space when the situation required it. In a perfect world, maybe everyone would live it the way we do. It's what friendship is supposed to be.

Through it all, we've remained playful with each other. Goldberg wrote of religious rituals that involve tickling. I don't know much about that, but I do feel sense of...rightness, that things are the way they're supposed to be, when we all play together.

One time in particular was memorable. We were watching a movie on the couch, Jan stretched out. Her belly was across my lap, her feet were in Monica's. We were treating her to a two point massage. I began to get a little playful and let me fingertips wander to her sensitive underarms. She jumped a couple of times and began to squirm a little. Coming out of her massage-induced haze, she looked up at me with a smile and whispered "Cut it out. You know how ticklish I am!" I responded by tapping a ticklish spot at the top of her ribs. She giggled softly, drawing her arm down, and said "Monica, help! He's tickling me!"

Monica smiled at me and said "You mean like this?" She then wiggled her fingernails down Jan's soles. I looked over to see that Monica had already scissored Jan's sensitive tootsies between her thighs. Jan was helpless. "Koochie koo!" Monica teased.

Jan squealed and buried her face in the pillow. I gave her ribs a few quick probes while Monica teased her toes. We then stopped and went back to her massage. We kept this up for a heavenly half hour, massaging for a few minutes and then beginning another tickle attack.

"How am I supposed to relax wondering when you're gonna tickle me next?" Jan whined playfully.

Monica responded by tickling the tops of Jan's feet, near her shins. Jan really goes crazy when this is done and began to buck as she giggled helplessly. "Please, not there!" she managed to squeal.

"Oh, don't be such a baby" Monica cooed. "Why not change places if you don't like it?"

I sensed what Monica had in mind. "Ok, Jan give me your feet and Monica will do your back and shoulders. I promise not to tickle your feet." I winked at Monica.

Not believing me but playing along, Jan changed places. We gave her a couple of minutes of blissful massage before getting mischievous. Monica played her fingertips along the back of Jan's sensitive neck, while I covertly trapped her feet and kept my promise by stroking the sensitive backs of her knees instead of her feet.

Jan just about exploded from the shock. We didn't give her any breaks this time and just playfully tickled her for a minute while Jan struggled and giggled, threatening and promising all sorts of rewards if we did stop and revenges if we didn't. I guess the problem with that kind of thing is that you know if you keep it up the person will still be promising the same things in five minutes. Where's the incentive? I guess sometimes you can eat your cake and have it too.

When we stopped, Jan relaxed down into us. After a few seconds of getting her breath she looked up at Monica menacingly and said "I think it's your turn to get massaged now!"

Monica smiled and only said "Ok." It was a silent understanding between them, Jan was going to try to get Monica back and Monica was going to resist showing any reaction. Jan secured Monica into position and began to massage.

Monica failed in her attempt to resist, miserably.

114

A minute into her group massage, Jan began to tease the tender skin at the base of Monica's wiggling toes. I stopped my portion of the massage and just watched. This was their game.

Monica exploded into laughter as Jan began to tease. "I'm not the one being held now, am I? I can do this for hours, you know! What was it you said to me? Oh yes: KOOCHIE KOOCHIE KOO!!!" Monica didn't bother asking for mercy. She hadn't shown any, and she had had me helping her to tickle Jan.

After a minute or so, Jan let up and both friends laughed. We went back to our group massage. Suddenly it occurred to me that it wasn't fair. Jan had been group tickled, but Monica hadn't. I used my fingertips to tease until I found a sensitive spot down near her kidneys. As Monica began to squirm, Jan resumed her tickling ministrations to her feet.

We then gave her the same treatment Jan had received. A few minutes of massaging was interrupted by a minute or two of tickling. It was like being in heaven, playful and blissful, all cares left behind. Well, maybe not <u>all</u> cares left behind. A half hour later, Jan said "You know Monica, it's not fair of us to hog all the pleasure while he does all the work. Pete hasn't been massaged yet." With mixed emotions and a fluttering stomach I got into position. It guess it's useless to deny destiny, and I guess I had dug my own grave. I had also loved doing it.

I don't remember what the movie was, it was hard to concentrate that night. A wise woman once said that television is for people whose real lives don't measure up. That night, and many since, mine did.

Tickle

Feather touch.
I giggle, jump
Squirm closer.
More, please.
Sensitive skin
Brought to life
My reaction is evoked
Beyond my control.
I can hide pain
Even smother an orgasm
But to this,
I am helpless.
Limbs move
Without my consent
Laughter and moans erupt
Through clenched teeth.
Oh, more, please.
I am trying to get away
It's too much
Too intense
I can't take this anymore.
Fingertips teasing my toes,
My ribs,
My soles and hips.
At the same time
Excitement is building
It feels too good
I love this
Love the hand
Gripping my ankle
Love the fingers
Torturing my foot
Love he who has become master
Of my every reaction
While begging him to stop
Somehow, I wish
For this to last forever
The ambiguity
Makes my head spin.
So close, so personal
What was in the past
Merely playful
Or annoying
Has become incredibly erotic
Under his skilled attention.
There's no turning back now.
I need it.

References and further reading

Claxton, G. (1975). Why can't we tickle ourselves? Perceptual and Motor Skills, 41, 335-338.

Comfort, A. (1972) The joy of sex. New York: Simon and Schuster.

Farrel, L. (1985). The touching truth about tickling. Mademoiselle, 91, 54.

Fridlund, A. J. & Loftus, J. M. (1990). Relations between tickling and humorous laughter: Preliminary support for the Darwin-Hecker hypothesis. Biological Psychology, 30, 141-150.

Goldberg, B. Z. (1958). The sacred fire: The story of sex in religion. New York: University Books.

Hivnor, R. (1949/1956). The ticklish acrobat. In Playbook: Five plays for a new theater (pp. 27-127). New York: New Directions Books.

Hoshikawa, T. (1991). Effects of attention and expectation on tickle sensation. Perceptual and Motor Skills, 72, 27-33.

Leuba, C. (1941). Tickling and laughter. Journal of Genetic Psychology, 58, 201-209.

Love, B. B. (1992). Encyclopedia of unusual sex practices. Fort Lee: Barricade Books.

Meyers, R. G., Landis, E. R., & Hayes, J. R. (1988). Law for the psychotherapist. New York: W. W. Norton.

Niremberg, S. A. (1991). Normal and pathological laughter in children. Clinical Pediatrics, 30(11), 630-632.

Orchnik, C. W. (1958). On tickling and stuttering. Psychoanalytic Review, 25-40.

Phillips, A. (1993). On kissing, tickling, and being bored. Cambridge: Harvard University Press.

Rossi, W. A. (1978). The sex life of the foot and shoe. New York: Ballantine Books.

Rueger, R. A. (1981) The joy of touch. New York: Wallaby Books.

Ruggieri, V., Milizia, M. & Angeli, F. (1985). Reaction to cutaneous (tickle) and sexual pleasure by normal and dermapathic subjects. Perceptual and Motor Skills, 61, 903-910.

Ruggieri, V., Milizia, M. & Romano, M. F. (1979). Effects of body image on tactile sensitivity to a tickle: A study in pregnancy. Perceptual and Motor Skills, 49, 555-563.

Ruggieri, V., & Milizia, M. (1983). Tickle perception
    as micro-experience of pleasure: Its phenomenology
    on different areas of the body and relation to
    cerebral dominance. Perceptual and Motor Skills,
    56, 903-914.
Ruggieri, V., Milizia, M., Sabatini, N. & Tosi, M. T.
    (1983). Body perception in relation to muscular
    tone at rest and tactile sensitivity to tickle.
    Perceptual and Motor Skills, 56, 799-806.
Ruggieri, V., Sabatini, N. & Milizia, M. (1983).
    Muscular tone at rest: Relationship with
    cutaneous pleasurable experience, an
    interpretation according to the dimensional
    approach to cerebral dominance.
Sabatini, N., Ruggieri, V., & Milizia, M. (1984).
    Barrier and penetration scores in relation to some
    objective and subjective somesthetic measures.
    Perceptual and Motor Skills, 59, 195-202.
Science Digest. (1984). Why are we ticklish?
    August, p. 20.
Scott, G. G. (1983). Erotic power: An exploration of
    dominance and submission. Seacaucus, NJ: Citadel
    Press.
Weisberg, P. (1976). Developmental differences in
    children's preferences for high- and low-arousing
    forms of contact stimulation. Child Development,
    46, 975-979.